YORK NOT

C000024648

# GULLIVER'S TRAVELS

JONATHAN SWIFT

## NOTES BY MARY SEWELL

 Longman

 York Press

YORK PRESS
322 Old Brompton Road, London SW5 9JH

PEARSON EDUCATION LIMITED
Edinburgh Gate, Harlow,
Essex CM20 2JE, United Kingdom
Associated companies, branches and representatives throughout the world

First published 1999
The new and fully revised edition first published 2003
Seventh impression 2017
10 9 8 7

ISBN: 978-0-582-77265-6

Designed by Michelle Cannatella
Illustrated by Neil Evans
Typeset by Land & Unwin (Data Sciences), Bugbrooke, Northamptonshire
Printed in Great Britain by Ashford Colour Press Ltd., Gosport, Hampshire

# CONTENTS

# PREFACE

York Notes are designed to give you a broader perspective on works of literature studied at GCSE and equivalent levels. With examination requirements changing in the twenty-first century, we have made a number of significant changes to this new series. We continue to help students to reach their own interpretations of the text but York Notes now have important extra-value new features.

You will discover that York Notes are genuinely interactive. The new **Checkpoint** features make sure that you can test your knowledge and broaden your understanding. You will also be directed to excellent websites, books and films where you can follow up ideas for yourself.

The **Resources** section has been updated and an entirely new section has been devoted to how to improve your grade. Careful reading and application of the principles laid out in the Resources section guarantee improved performance.

The **Detailed summaries** include an easy-to-follow skeleton structure of the story-line, while the section on **Language and style** has been extended to offer an in-depth discussion of the writer's techniques.

The Contents page shows the structure of this study guide. However, there is no need to read from the beginning to the end as you would with a novel, play or poem. Use the Notes in the way that suits you. Our aim is to help you with your understanding of the work, not to dictate how you should learn.

Our authors are practising English teachers and examiners who have used their experience to offer a whole range of **Examiner's secrets** – useful hints to encourage exam success.

The General Editor of this series is John Polley, Senior GCSE Examiner and former Head of English at Harrow Way Community School, Andover.

The author of these Notes is Mary Sewell MA, B Ed, senior examiner for GCSE literature. She is a tutor with the Open University, and delivers in-service training for teachers.

The text used in these Notes is the Penguin Classics edition, 1985, edited by Peter Dixon and John Chalker with an introduction by Michael Foot.

## PART ONE

# INTRODUCTION

## HOW TO STUDY A NOVEL

A novelist starts with a story that examines a situation and the actions of particular characters. Remember that authors are not photographers, and that a novel never resembles real life exactly. Ultimately, a novel represents a view of the world that has been created in the author's imagination.

There are six features of a novel:

1. THE STORY: this is the series of events, deliberately organised by the writer to test the characters

2. THE CHARACTERS: the people who have to respond to the events of the story. Since they are human, they can be good or bad, clever or stupid, likeable or detestable, etc. They may change too!

3. THE VIEWPOINT/VOICE: who is telling the story. The viewpoint may come from one of the characters, or from an omniscient (all-seeing) narrator, which allows the novelist to write about the perspectives of all the characters

4. THE THEMES: these are the underlying messages, or meanings, of the novel

5. THE SETTING: this concerns the time and place that the author has chosen for the story

6. THE LANGUAGE AND STYLE: these are the words that the author has used to influence our understanding of the novel

To arrive at the fullest understanding of a novel, you need to read it several times. In this way, you can see how all the choices the author has made add up to a particular view of life, and develop your own ideas about it.

The purpose of these York Notes is to help you understand what the novel is about and to enable you to make your own interpretation. Do not expect the study of a novel to be neat and easy: novels are chosen for examination purposes, not written for them!

 **DID YOU KNOW?**
Although something like the novel existed in ancient cultures, literary historians usually identify the start of the novel (as we think of it today) in the eighteenth century.

## AUTHOR – LIFE AND WORKS

## CONTEXT

**1667** Jonathan Swift is born 30 November

**1672–82** Attends Kilkenny Grammar School

**1682–9** Attends Trinity College in Dublin

**1689–95** Employed as secretary to Sir William Temple

**1694** Ordained as a priest in Ireland

**1696–99** Returns to work for Sir William and meets Esther Johnson (Stella)

**1704** Publishes *Tale of a Tub* and *Battle of the Books* anonymously

**1710** Returns to London; becomes politically active for the Tories

**1713** Becomes Dean of St Patrick's Cathedral in Dublin

**1720** Begins writing *Gulliver's Travels*

**1726** *Gulliver's Travels* is published

**1727** *Gulliver's Travels* is translated into French, Dutch and German

**1728** Esther Johnson (Stella) dies

**1729** *A Modest Proposal* is published

**1745** Swift dies 19 October

---

**1642–6** Civil war between the Roundheads and the Cavaliers

**1660** Charles II takes the throne

**1666** The Great Fire of London

**1667** *Paradise Lost* by John Milton is published

**1678–84** *Pilgrim's Progress* by John Bunyan is published

**1685** Charles II dies, James II succeeds

**1687** Newton publishes his first book

**1689** William and Mary take the throne

**1699** Gulliver's first voyage

**1701–13** The war of the Spanish Succession

**1702** Anne takes the throne

**1707** Great Britain is created

**1714** George I succeeds Anne

**1715** Gulliver's final return home

**1721** Walpole becomes prime minister

**1727** George I dies, George II succeeds

**1744** Death of writer Alexander Pope

**1755** Samuel Johnson publishes his *Dictionary of the English Language*

## SETTING AND BACKGROUND

### THE LIFE OF JONATHAN SWIFT

#### Early years

Jonathan Swift was born in Dublin on 30 November 1667. His father died before he was born and as a consequence he was raised in Cumbria for the first three years of his life. The family had no money and it was Godwin Swift, one of Swift's uncles, who ensured that he was educated. He first went to Kilkenny School and later Trinity College at Dublin. Godwin died in 1688 and Swift then went to work for Sir William Temple in Surrey as his private secretary. Sir William was a retired diplomat, now a leading member of the Liberal Party. It was here that Swift became interested in politics and political power and became ambitious. Here he composed three of his most famous satires, 'A Tale of a Tub' (1704), 'The Battle of the Books' (1704), and 'Discourse concerning the Mechanical Operation of the Spirit' (1704). It was during this time that Swift first became ill with Ménière's disease, an illness which caused giddiness and vomiting. He tried returning to Ireland, hoping a change of climate would help his condition, but later returned to work for Sir William. In 1695 he met Esther Johnson, whom he referred to as Stella. At this time, Stella was only fifteen years of age, and quickly became friends with Swift, who was also her tutor. This was a friendship that was to endure a lifetime.

#### Religion and politics

In 1694 Swift was ordained a priest, and he became Dean of St Patrick's Cathedral in 1713. After Sir William's death in 1699, Stella moved over to Ireland and stayed near Swift. There is some evidence that they secretly married in 1716, but the relationship was one of friendship. They saw each other every day and Swift wrote to her using intimate messages. He always composed a verse for her birthday.

In 1701 Swift, whose upbringing had been Whig (despite a Royalist and High Church background), wrote a pamphlet praising the Whigs (or Liberal) leaders. It was called 'A Discourse of the Contests and Dissensions between the Nobles and the Commons in

**DID YOU KNOW?**
Swift wrote a number of intimate letters to Esther Johnson, entitled *Journal to Stella.*

**DID YOU KNOW?**
Swift was editor of the official Tory paper, *The Examiner.*

**DID YOU KNOW?**

It is generally thought that *Gulliver's Travels* took more than six years to write.

**DID YOU KNOW?**

*Gulliver's Travels* was published anonymously at first.

Athens and Rome'. It was this pamphlet that made his political reputation. Swift experienced a tension between his political and religious beliefs and eventually, when the Whig ministry of Godolphin fell in 1710, he changed his political allegiance and became a Tory. Swift wrote some deeply religious pamphlets at this time such as 'Sentiments of a Church of England Man', and the ironic 'Argument against Abolishing Christianity', and became the author of a Tory journal 'The Examiner' and 'The Conduct of the Allies'.

### Later writing

In 1726 *Gulliver's Travels* was published and became a huge success. One of Swift's friends wrote to him and said: 'From the highest to the lowest it is universally read, from the cabinet-council to the nursery'.

His later writings included *Short View of the State of Ireland* (1728), *A Modest Proposal* (1729), *Verses on the Death of Dr Swift* (1731) and *The Legion Club* (1736). Jonathan Swift was found to be suffering from a brain tumour that caused madness in the last three years of his life. His illness worsened and he died on 19 October 1745. Swift was buried under his own epitaph, which was written in Latin. W. B. Yeats translated it:

> Swift has sailed to his rest;
>
> Savage indignation there
>
> Cannot lacerate his breast,
>
> Imitate him if you dare,
>
> World-besotted traveller; he
>
> Served human liberty.

### INSPIRATION FOR MYSTERIOUS LANDS

The imaginary locations for *Gulliver's Travels* are:

1. Lilliput

2. Brobdingnag

3. Laputa

④ Balnibarbi

⑤ Glubbdubdrib

⑥ Luggnagg

⑦ The land of Houyhnhnms

Swift included two maps in his earlier version of *Gulliver's Travels*, and it was thought by readers that the lands of Lilliput and Brobdingnag actually did exist. We know that Swift had read *New Voyage round the World* in 1717, a tale of a mariner's voyages fighting dangerous natural phenomena. Swift loved travel and had explored most of Ireland. *Gulliver's Travels* is set in the South Seas or Pacific Ocean. We are given vague instructions as to actually where. In Lilliput we are told the latitude but not the longitude and we are left to presume the islands lie in the Indian Ocean. In Brobdingnag it is a monsoon that takes the ship off course from the Molucca islands into the Pacific. The journey reaches an imaginary continent – we must remember that this area remained unexplored in 1725. Conveniently another storm drives the ship to Laputa in the North Pacific, and the land of the Houyhnhnms is said to be 10° south of the Cape of Good Hope, or 45° south east of Madagascar. The maps in these Notes are the original maps of *Gulliver's Travels*. The locations of the novel are imaginary and *Gulliver's Travels* is heavily satirical and ironical. We should consider the influences on Swift's own background which we find reflected in these mysterious lands, and it is absolutely necessary to have a little understanding of his life and times in order to understand the full implications of the novel.

## The Church

At this time humankind was thought to be 'good'; individuals were motivated by sympathy, friendship and benevolence. It was thought that people were naturally logical, rational and virtuous in the same way that we feel today that we are liberal, generous and humanitarian.

However, Swift did not agree with these views. He saw humankind as savage, driven by greed and lust, envy and avarice. This view, that people succumbed to the seven deadly sins if they were not communicant members of the Church, is indeed severe, even for Swift's times. Preachers such as John Wesley found in *Gulliver's*

**CHECK THE FILM**

*The Madness of King George* (1994) depicts a similar kind of illness to that of Jonathan Swift. This illness had periods of madness interspersed with periods of very stark reality. The film will also help set the historical background for the novel.

**DID YOU KNOW?**

The first two voyages may be read simply as a story for children. However, Gulliver's account of the land of Houyhnhnms is no fairy tale.

*Travels* proof for the theory of original sin, which was the innate depravity of man, depicted by Adam eating the forbidden fruit.

In Swift's novel we have plenty of evidence of moral criticism, but ironically for a book written by a clergyman, little evidence of religious faith. Swift believed in the Anglican Church, established after 1688, which held a position of religious freedom for all, demonstrating neither a preference for Catholics nor Dissenters (Puritans).

After 1629, King Charles I dissolved Parliament as he prepared for a civil war between the Cavaliers (Scots Catholics and English Royalists) and the Roundheads (Scots Presbyterians and English Republicans). Oliver Cromwell, a Puritan who ruled England for ten years as Lord Protector, led the Roundheads.

In 1660, Charles II was crowned. This period is called the Restoration (i.e. the restoration of the British monarchy). The parliament was made up of Cavaliers, Tory squires and old Roundheads. There was some religious persecution of Dissenters. The Tory party found itself opposed by a Whig party who believed in religious toleration, especially for Protestants.

### War with France

There were attempts to restore James, as a Catholic, to the English throne. War with France was inevitable to prevent Jacobitism (i.e. support of James). The duke of Marlborough led Protestant Europe through the War of the Spanish Succession (1701–13). This alliance of Whigs and Tories shared the responsibility for the government's money. War is expensive, and the English people simply wanted peace. The Treaty of Utrecht was therefore drawn up. It was during this time that Swift changed his political allegiance from Whig to Tory.

### Situation in Ireland

Ireland was at this time a poor country consisting mainly of Catholics who were anti-English. Indeed, over the decades, Ireland supported England's enemies in Spain and France. About once a year the Irish organised a rebellion and soldiers from England were sent to quell the riots. Each year some of the English stayed behind and over the years Ireland was governed by absentee landlords. Ireland was denied any trading, and ruled by corrupt second-rate ambassadors, none of whom were Irish. Swift, who believed in order and authority, saw Ireland as a land of neglect and decay. He felt he was living among 'beggars, thieves, oppressors, fools and knaves'. He firmly believed that the princes should protect their subjects and that the subjects in their turn should return a debt of loyalty to their princes. Swift felt that the Anglo-Irish had been denied their rights under the Revolution Settlement. Swift was particularly critical of Walpole's government and he produced pamphlets criticising matters in Ireland in the 1720s – the same time he wrote *Gulliver's Travels*.

## Women

Although Swift was a clergyman and a bachelor, three women had an influence on his life and his career. The first was Jane Waring whom Swift called Varina. He proposed marriage to her in 1695; she refused him but later changed her mind. However, the refusal had hurt Swift's pride and he decided not to marry.

At Moor Park, Swift was to educate Esther Johnson. Their friendship grew and Stella, as Swift called her, followed him to Ireland. Stella became his lifelong friend. When she became sick and died, Swift was so upset he could not attend the funeral.

During his visits to London in 1707–9, Swift met the third woman in his life. Esther Van Lomriyh was the centre of Anglo-Irish society. Swift called her Vanessa. Vanessa fell passionately in love with him and followed him to Ireland in 1714. Swift could not return the passion. Vanessa died in 1723 after a stormy love affair. Swift had written a poem 'Cadenus and Vanessa' which indicated the inequality of this love affair.

 **DID YOU KNOW?**
Walpole was a Whig and had great political power. He is considered to have been the first prime minister of England (1721–42), even though the title did not become official till 1905.

 **CHECK THE BOOK**
In *A Modest Proposal* (1729), Swift uses irony to argue on behalf of the poor people of Ireland. In it, he proposes that the children of the poor should be raised for slaughter as food for the rich.

## PART TWO

## SUMMARIES

# GENERAL SUMMARY

Gulliver's Travels is a satirical novel. It works on two levels; the first a simple but exciting fairy-tale, the second a comment on Swift's life and background.

## PART I

**DID YOU KNOW?**
Two maps were included in the earlier version of *Gulliver's Travels* and readers thought the lands Lilliput and Brobdingnag actually did exist!

In his first voyage to Lilliput, Gulliver is shipwrecked. His captors are one twelfth of his own size but they manage to secure him as their prisoner. The social/political background of these people is similar to that found in England. Part I portrays the reigns of Queen Anne and George I. Gulliver is impeached and tried for treason, rather like the Earl of Oxford and Viscount Bolingbroke.

## PART II

Once again, Gulliver is shipwrecked and accidentally abandoned by his shipmates, in what vaguely appears to be North America. This time the natives are twelve times bigger than Gulliver. He is adopted as a pet and exhibited as a sideshow. Once again Swift uses Gulliver to make a political comment. This time he represents an eighteenth-century Englishman attempting to show morality, courage, honesty and realism to a benevolent though cynical giant monarch.

## PART III

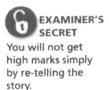

**EXAMINER'S SECRET**
You will not get high marks simply by re-telling the story.

Pirates capture Gulliver and leave him on some small islands which we are told rather vaguely are near to Japan. This journey is different as Gulliver actually flies, on a flying island called Laputa. People obsessed by science, maths and astronomy populate this island. These people bully the people of Balnibarbi, who live beneath them and literally in their shadow. Swift uses this to make a comment on the ill-governed Britain of George I.

Swift cleverly shows us how humankind's claim to be rational is false, and gives us numerous examples to illustrate this. From this island Gulliver visits Balnibarbi; on this island he witnesses bizarre practices and scientific experiments  We are then taken to Luggnagg where the people, Struldbruggs, are doomed to everlasting senility, a terrifying sight of physical decay and mental infirmity.

## PART IV

The voyage in Part IV returns us to a Utopian state, a land populated by two contrasting species. The Houyhnhnms are intelligent, superior, sensitive and empathetic, but have horselike rather than human form. The opposite are the Yahoos who are dirty, savage, wild and primitive, but are human in form. However, the Houyhnhnms regard Gulliver as a Yahoo, and Gulliver is very sensitive of this. This journey affects Gulliver most deeply. On his return he seeks out conversations with his own horses and sees humankind as savage and barbaric just as the Yahoos were. Gulliver has become a man who has seen perfection and now seeks it everywhere.

**CHECK THE FILM**
Some features included in the Channel 4 film are not present in the text. The bizarre commitment of Gulliver to an asylum and his subsequent trial by the doctors and rescue by his wife are not part of the original text.

ow take a break!

# DETAILED SUMMARIES

## I.1 – Arrival at Lilliput

① Gulliver narrates his background.

② He begins a voyage but is soon shipwrecked and arrives on Lilliput.

③ The Lilliputians drug Gulliver and take him to a temple.

**CHECKPOINT 1**

What is the point of Gulliver's description of his background?

Lemuel Gulliver begins his narrative with details of his childhood and training as a surgeon. We are almost catapulted into details of Gulliver's life. After being unable to make a living on land he sets sail on 4 May 1699 from Bristol in the *Antelope*. Unfortunately the ship 'to the north-west of Van Diemen's Land' (p. 54) is shipwrecked and all Lemuel's companions lost. He wades ashore and falls asleep, but when he awakes he finds his hair and body are tied to the ground and he is unable to move. To his surprise he sees 'a human creature not six inches high' (p. 56).

**CHECKPOINT 2**

What is your first impression of the people of Lilliput?

He attempts to escape but a volley of tiny arrows dissuades him from moving further. The inhabitants erect a stage and a tiny orator addresses the crowd. Gulliver fails to understand what is being said but is fed on meat and wine, which have been drugged, and subsequently falls asleep. The Lilliputians take Gulliver to their city on a specially constructed vehicle drawn by 'Fifteen hundred of the Emperor's largest horses, each about four inches and a half high' (p. 61). He is settled in a disused temple, where he is able to walk a little and sleep.

### The Lilliputians

The details about the diminutive people of Lilliput add to the credibility of the story. Jonathan Swift has taken us into this magical world of miniature Lilliput, where tiny beings, who are described by Gulliver as being 'excellent mathematicians' (p. 61), live in a hierarchical state similar to that with which Gulliver is familiar.

This chapter is a largely innocent narrative and inspires the reader's confidence.

**CHECKPOINT 3**

How do the people of Lilliput react to Gulliver?

## 1.2 – Gulliver on show

● **Gulliver meets the Emperor.**

● **Gulliver wins over the court.**

● **He is put on public show but is well looked after.**

The chapter opens with an account of the way in which Gulliver dealt with his bodily functions and of his meeting with the Emperor, whose features are described as 'strong and masculine' (p. 65). Although Gulliver tries several European languages, this is unsuccessful and the pair are left to communicate with signs and gestures. Gulliver and the imperial court find means of communicating and really get to know each other. Gulliver demonstrates an act of mercy by releasing six ruffians, after first pretending to eat one of them. This gesture is well received by the court. Six hundred beds are combined to make Gulliver a bed – Gulliver's needs are all covered in this chapter.

**CHECKPOINT 4**

How much do you think the Emperor trusts Gulliver?

Gulliver, the 'Man-Mountain' (p. 69), is put on view to the public. The Emperor has to make a law banning people from coming to see Gulliver more than once because it affects their work. Two officers search Gulliver and make a list of his possessions; his sword and pistols are taken from him. The reader is reassured as to his welfare.

## 1.3 – The Court of Lilliput

● **The court is described.**

● **Gulliver wins the Lilliputians' trust and is granted more freedom.**

● **The Lilliputians exploit Gulliver's size and strength.**

**GLOSSARY**

**Van Dieman's Land** present-day Tasmania

This chapter is full of satire and irony (see **Satire and irony** in **Themes**).

The opening paragraph describes how the boys and girls 'play at hide and seek' in Gulliver's hair (p. 73), and goes on to describe the satirical court where political 'candidates' (p. 74) perform tricks of rope-dancing and jump like acrobats. The people of Lilliput gain the Emperor's approval by demonstrating an acrobatic skill and therefore becoming courtiers or by leaping or crawling under a stick and winning a silken thread.

**CHECKPOINT 5**

Consider what Jonathan Swift is trying to tell us about promotions in this description.

**? DID YOU KNOW?**

The Lilliputians represent the Whig party of England.

Gulliver helps miniature horses perform by tying his handkerchief to sticks, making a platform for military displays, until a horse's hoof goes through the handkerchief and Gulliver considers it unsafe. The Emperor is so impressed that he is persuaded to grant Gulliver more freedom of movement. Two days later, Gulliver is requested to 'stand like a colossus, with my legs as far asunder as I conveniently could' (p. 77) whilst the army marchs between them. The government debates Gulliver's freedom and, as there is only one objection, he is granted his liberty after swearing to the eight conditions. Note the bizarre ritual Gulliver has to undergo in order to swear his obedience to the 'articles and conditions' (p. 78). The seventh sentences Gulliver to hard labour in his leisure hours. Gulliver is allowed enough food to support 1,728 Lilliputians.

CHECKPOINT 6

Who objects to Gulliver's freedom?

The eight 'articles'

Gulliver must:

1. Not leave Lilliput without permission
2. Give two hours' warning of a visit
3. Keep to the main roads as he walks
4. Take care as he moves
5. Carry messages when required
6. Defend Lilliput from its enemies
7. Help with the building by lifting heavy stones
8. Measure the kingdom

This chapter reflects King George's court under the Walpole government.

## 1.4 – An interview with Reldresal

1. Gulliver descibes the capital city of Mildendo.
2. Gulliver discusses Lilliput's politics with Reldresal.
3. Gulliver agrees to help Lilliput in their war with Blefescu.

The capital Mildendo is described in detail by Gulliver when he visits the Emperor's palace.

This chapter gives us an account of England and its historical factions – e.g. the 'bloody war' is the war of the Spanish Succession (see **Setting and background**).

CHECKPOINT 7

Note the description of the city. What effect does this have?

> **Political parties**
>
> Reldresal, Principal Secretary of Private Affairs, interviews Gulliver, and tells him the political problems facing Lilliput. The two main parties are:
>
> 1. *Tramecksan* (the High-Heels), the largest and more traditional party; refers to the Tories of Swift's own time
>
> 2. *Slamecksan* (the Low-Heels), who are currently favoured by the Emperor and are in power; refers to the Whigs of Swift's own time
>
> At this time Charles II favoured the Whigs, but the Crown Prince kept in favour with both parties and was said to 'hobble' with one heel higher than the other.

---

**CHECKPOINT 8**

How are the Big-Endians treated?

---

**? DID YOU KNOW?**
Big-Endians and Little-Endians are current terms for the ordering (arrangement) of computer bytes.

---

Blefuscu is the one rival empire to Lilliput in this story. Blefuscu has supported the cause of the 'Big-Endians' against the 'Little-Endians'. The Big-Endians supported Blefuscu in their war against Lilliput. The Big-Endians were like the Catholics in England at this time, not allowed to hold high office. Reldresal tells Gulliver that they are in danger from an invasion and Gulliver readily agrees to help.

## I.5 – Fire at the Palace

1. Gulliver helps in the war against Blefuscu.

2. The relationship between Gulliver and the Emperor breaks down.

Gulliver swims across the eight-hundred-yard channel between Lilliput and Blefuscu, hooks up the Blefuscudian fleet to cables and tows it back over to Lilliput. As a reward, Gulliver is made a Duke '*Nardac*', but decides not to help the Emperor any further to completely destroy Blefuscu. He claims he would 'never be an

instrument of bringing a free and brave people into slavery' (p. 89).
Note the way Gulliver's services are responded to by both the
Emperor and the Empress. Gulliver begins to lose favour in Lilliput
and he remarks 'Of so little weight are the greatest services to
princes' (p. 89), indicating a break down in his relationship with the
Emperor.

A treaty is arranged with Blefuscu, but Gulliver's friendly attitude
towards the people of Blefuscu, and his display of strength, seem to
make matters worse.

**CHECK THE FILM**
Gulliver's urinating on the fire is omitted from the Channel 4 film.

### Putting out the fire

Further offence is caused when Gulliver puts out a fire in the
palace by urinating on the flames. The incident of the palace fire
is thought to represent the Treaty of Utrecht, where
Bolingbroke and Oxford used illegal means to extinguish a
conflagration.

The Emperor and Gulliver part coolly, as a result of the influence of
Gulliver's enemies who thought him guilty of treason.

**CHECKPOINT 9**

What causes the change in Gulliver's relationship with the Emperor?

## 1.6 – Local customs

**① Gulliver describes the Lilliputian customs and education.**

**② We learn about Gulliver's own domestic details.**

This chapter has to be carefully considered; some parts seem a description of Utopia, others a very tongue-in-cheek commentary.

Gulliver gives us a detailed account of some of the customs of the Lilliputians. We learn that they write diagonally and that their dead are buried with their heads downwards. In recruitment for employment, good character is more creditable than high ability.

---

**Lilliputian law**

Note the differences between our systems of justice and that in Lilliput:

- People are punished for making false accusations

- Embezzlers are executed

- People who demonstrate ingratitude are punished with death

- Atheists are not allowed public service

- Law-abiding people in Lilliput are rewarded with special honours

---

**CHECKPOINT 10**

What happens to these children later?

Gulliver also deals with education. Young Lilliputians are educated in single-sex schools with slight differences between the boys' and girls' education. Children on farms are not taught in school at all.

Gulliver's domestic details are given to us. We learn 'Two hundred sempstresses were employed to make me shirts', and 'three hundred cooks' (p. 100). This huge expense was recalled by Flimnap, the Lord High Treasurer to the Emperor, who claimed Gulliver had cost 'a million and a half of sprugs' (p. 101). This combined with a rumour about the close relationship between Gulliver and Flimnap's wife led to rift between Gulliver and the Emperor.

## 1.7 – Escape from Lilliput

**1** Gulliver is the victim of a plot.

**2** He is sentenced to death for treason.

**3** Gulliver escapes to Blefuscu.

*Gulliver*

Gulliver, having given the reader an insight into the laws and customs of Lilliput, is about to experience them. He is the victim of a plot to impeach him for treason. He is accused of four main crimes:

**1** Urinating on the palace

**2** Refusing to crush Blefuscu

**3** Showing friendliness towards the enemy

**4** Planning to travel to and side with Blefuscu

The council delivers its punishment and Gulliver is told he is to be blinded and then starved to death. This would make his carcass 'more than half diminished' (p. 108) and thereby be less of a health hazard as it decays. Note the changes in Gulliver's attitude towards the society of Lilliput.

Three days later the impeachment is to be read to Gulliver and then the sentence carried out. Gulliver decides not to stand 'trial' before a court that has already decided his fate! Consider the irony in 'to signify the great *lenity* and favour of his Majesty and Council' (pp. 108–9). He wades across the channel and is warmly received in Blefuscu, where they hold a reception 'which was suitable to the generosity of so great a prince' (p. 111).

> **CHECKPOINT 11**
>
> List the factors that lead to a worsening of the relationship between Gulliver and the Emperor.

> **CHECKPOINT 12**
>
> Do you think that the impeachment is unfair?

## I.8 – Homecoming

1. Gulliver finds a boat.

2. The Lilliputians demand Gulliver's return but are refused.

3. Gulliver is rescued by an English ship and returns home.

4. Gulliver sets sail once again.

**CHECKPOINT 13**

Has Gulliver's attitude changed towards people in authority? If so, how?

**CHECKPOINT 14**

Compare the ways in which the Emperor of Blefuscu and the Emperor of Lilliput treat Gulliver.

Three days after arriving in Blefuscu, Gulliver finds a 'real boat' (p. 111). He manages to drag it ashore with the help of twenty Blefuscudian war ships. Meanwhile the Lilliputians send a message to Blefuscu, and demand that Gulliver be returned, 'bound hand and foot, to be punished as a traitor' (p. 113). The Monarch of Blefuscu replies saying that Gulliver's return is impossible. He offers Gulliver his 'gracious protection' (p. 114), but Gulliver's faith in promises has dwindled. Gulliver wants to take home a dozen Blefuscudians, but instead takes sheep and cattle.

Gulliver sets sail on 24 September 1701, and after two days is picked up by an English ship. Note the coincidences of the upturned boat and the English vessel returning home. Gulliver has to show the captain the miniature sheep and cattle to convince him of his story. Nearly seven months later he arrives home, on 13 April 1792, and makes a living by showing his miniature sheep.

Two months later, after speculating about whether to breed the tiny sheep for their wool, he sets sail on another adventure. Gulliver conveniently omits to mention his family's reaction to his voyage. We are only told that 'I took leave of my wife, and boy and girl, with tears on both sides' (p. 117). This lack of detail in Gulliver's homecoming contrasts dramatically with the detailed descriptions Gulliver has given of his journey to Lilliput.

Now take a break!

## ABOUT WHOM/WHAT?

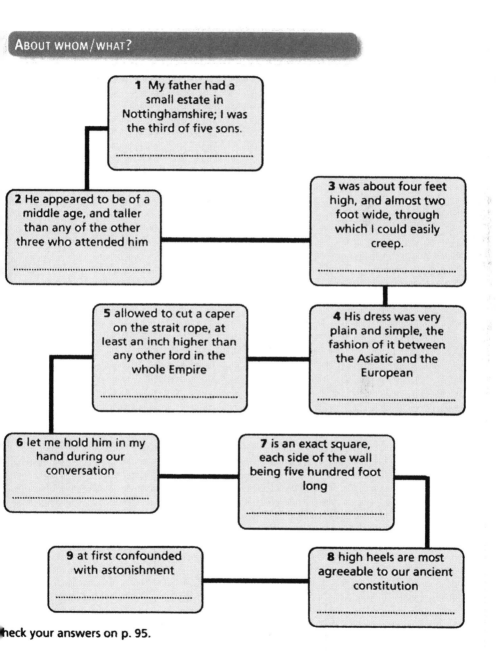

**1** My father had a small estate in Nottinghamshire; I was the third of five sons.

..................................................

**2** He appeared to be of a middle age, and taller than any of the other three who attended him

..................................................

**3** was about four feet high, and almost two foot wide, through which I could easily creep.

..................................................

**5** allowed to cut a caper on the strait rope, at least an inch higher than any other lord in the whole Empire

..................................................

**4** His dress was very plain and simple, the fashion of it between the Asiatic and the European

..................................................

**6** let me hold him in my hand during our conversation

..................................................

**7** is an exact square, each side of the wall being five hundred foot long

..................................................

**9** at first confounded with astonishment

..................................................

**8** high heels are most agreeable to our ancient constitution

..................................................

heck your answers on p. 95.

## II.1 – Arrival in Brobdingnag

**1** **Gulliver sets sail again.**

**2** **His shipmates abandon him.**

**3** **A giant man takes Gulliver home.**

In only one chapter, spanning two months, we are moved from the miniature world into a world of giants. Travelling in the *Adventurer*, Gulliver leaves Cornwall on 20 June 1702, and is blown off course and lands in the North Pacific on 16 June 1703. The nautical detail adds to the 'realism' of the journal. Gulliver goes ashore to find water but is abandoned by his shipmates who are chased by 'a huge creature walking after them in the sea' (p. 123). Gulliver turns to run away, but finds himself in a cornfield forty feet high, which is about to be harvested by more of these huge men. Note how Gulliver's 'curiosity' (p. 123) leads him again into trouble.

### At home with the giants

One of the giants takes Gulliver home with him to show to his wife. The handkerchief used to make a platform for the military display is now used to wrap around Gulliver. The farmer is convinced Gulliver is a 'rational creature' (p. 127), but his wife is afraid at first and only when Gulliver displays good manners and amusing tricks does she relax and breastfeed her infant, which Gulliver describes as 'nauseous' (p. 130).

Gulliver has several terrifying experiences in the company of the cat, infant and small boy. He is awoken from sleep by two rats and is forced to slay one of them. Gulliver describes how he 'discharged the necessities of nature' (p. 133). Gulliver's physical needs are obviously to be a major theme. Compare the detailed account in Part I, Chapter 1 with this one.

 **CHECK THE NET**
Search the Internet for James Gillray (1757–1815) – a well-known cartoonist. See if you can find his illustration of the land of Brondingnag and find out who he is satirising.

## II.2 – Glumdalclitch

**1** Glumdalclitch looks after Gulliver.

**2** Gulliver is taken to the capital.

Glumdalclitch, the nine-year-old daughter of the family, looks after Gulliver, whom she calls '*Grildrig*'. Gulliver says: 'To her I chiefly owe my preservation in that country: we never parted while I was there' (p. 134).

> **On show again**
>
> Glumdalclitch's father decides to show Gulliver as an exhibit and he is taken in a little padded box to the town where he is put onto a table to perform to the audience. Note the way Gulliver is placed high upon the table to perform just as the Lilliputians performed for Gulliver. Gulliver's appearances in public in Lilliput displayed his strength and his capacity for power and protection. In Brobdingnag his public appearances are just the opposite and the reader feels Gulliver's vulnerability.

**? DID YOU KNOW?**
Gulliver's nickname 'Grildrig' means 'manikin', and 'Glumdalclitch' means 'little nurse'.

**DID YOU KNOW?**

For about a hundred years until the mid-twentieth century, 'freak shows' were a popular form of entertainment.

Eventually the two-month tour ends in Lorbrulgrud, the capital of this country, as Gulliver becomes ill. During the tour Gulliver is taught the language by Glumdalclitch, with whom he is forming an affectionate relationship. In Lilliput Gulliver's relationships were with people in power: politicians and ambassadors. In Brobdingnag his relationships are warmer and more intimate, especially with Glumdalclitch.

## II.3 – The Palace

① Gulliver stays at the court.

② Gulliver must contend with a dwarf.

③ Gulliver fights off giant wasps and flies.

**CHECKPOINT 15**

Compare the various reactions to Gulliver in this chapter.

Gulliver becomes further weakened, but his health is saved when he is bought by the Queen. Glumdalclitch is also to stay at court to look after Gulliver. Note how quickly Gulliver settles down to a comfortable life in the Palace.

> **Changing opinions**
>
> Note the change in Gulliver's attitude from being defensive of the English Court to agreeing that English Lords and Ladies are ridiculous.
>
> Consider the change in Gulliver's own attitude to his own size: 'the horror I had first conceived from their bulk and aspect was so far worn off' (p. 146).

Gulliver confides in the Queen that his health is not good. The Queen, 'surprised at so much wit and good sense in so diminutive an animal' (p. 141), takes him under her protection. The King at first sees him as a '*splacknuck*' and then decides he is a clockwork toy. Three court scholars are called to question Gulliver and decide he is just a '*lusus naturae*' (p. 143) – a freak of nature. A house is made for Gulliver and he dines with the Queen and converses with the King. Gulliver is embarrassed by the King's observations on human society to begin with but later becomes angry at the lack of sensitivity.

Gulliver is dropped into a bowl of cream by his enemy, the dwarf – who is later 'soundly whipped' (p. 147). He then fights off huge flies and wasps, keeping some of the wasp stings to take back to England as a souvenir.

## II.4 – Local descriptions

**1** **Brobdingnag is described.**

**2** **Gulliver travels there but dislikes the city.**

Brobdingnag is described as a huge continent rather like North America; it is cut off on one side by stormy seas and on another by a thirty-mile-high range of mountains. Note Gulliver's obsession with relating everything to size.

Gulliver travels in a specially made 'travelling closet' (p. 152). He experiences 'the most horrible spectacles that ever an European eye

**CHECKPOINT 16**

Why do you think that the city is so graphically described? Is there a similar passage in the first journey?

beheld' (p. 151) and describes cancer, lice, beggars and blisters. He is not impressed with either the King's palace or the chief temple but he is taken by the King's kitchen, 'a noble building' (p. 153).

**? DID YOU KNOW?**
St Paul's cathedral was built during Swift's lifetime after the original cathedral was badly damaged in the Great Fire of London in 1666.

> ## Comparisons with home
>
> Note the comparison in this chapter to England. The coach is compared to Westminster Hall, the chief temple to the steeple of Salisbury Cathedral, the King's oven to St Paul's cupola in London.

## II.5 – Adventures and accidents

1 Gulliver describes a number of accidents.

2 Gulliver visits the Maids of Honour.

3 Gulliver is abducted by a monkey.

In the first part of the chapter, Gulliver describes how his 'littleness' gets him into 'several ridiculous and troublesome accidents' (p. 154):

1 A dwarf bombards him with apples.

2 He is struck by giant hailstones.

3 A spaniel picks him up.

4 He is nearly caught by a kite.

5 He falls into a molehill.

6 He hurts his leg on a snail's shell.

7 He is pecked at by birds.

> ## A comment on morality
>
> In addition, Gulliver is laid naked on the bosoms of the Maids of Honour, by which he is 'much disgusted' (p. 157). Jonathan Swift is making a comment on Court morals and is accusing them of immorality and sexual licence.

**CHECK THE FILM**
The Maids of Honour scene is omitted from the 1996 film.

The next episode deals with the execution of a murderer, which Gulliver describes graphically but in a detached way: 'The veins and arteries spurted up such a prodigious quantity of blood' (p. 159). The Queen, in an attempt to divert Gulliver, has a boat and a trough made for him to sail in. However, this too results in misadventure: Gulliver is abducted by a monkey, which attempts to feed him but nearly chokes him, and the chapter ends with his encounter with some cow-dung.

## II. 6 – An interview with the King

1 Gulliver makes some furniture.

2 The King interviews him.

3 The King is unimpressed by Gulliver's account of England.

The chapter opens with an amusing account of Gulliver making a comb out of the King's beard, and chairs out of the Queen's hair. Gulliver uses his inventiveness to amuse the reader and once again, the domestic detail of Gulliver's life reminds us of his tiny size. Gulliver also learns techniques that make it possible to play the enormous spinet.

The King, in a series of interviews, asks a number of innocent yet searching questions. Gulliver attempts to support the argument for the worth of the undersized by referring to the superior 'industry, art and sagacity' of bees and ants (p. 167) and the King's opinion of Gulliver improves.

**DID YOU KNOW?**

Gulliver's views here are not the same as those of Swift.

Gulliver then goes on to describe the English Parliament, 'the most august assembly in Europe' (p. 168). First he describes the House of Peers where there is 'valour, conduct and fidelity' (p. 167), then the House of Commons which represents 'the wisdom of the whole nation' (p. 168). The King then questions him on:

- The Lords

- The Commoners

- Justice

- The treasury

- The army

- Gaming

---

### The last century in England

Gulliver concludes with a historical account of his country over the last hundred years. Jonathan Swift builds up this scene that was meant to inspire confidence and then shocks the reader with the King's final verdict. The King, apparently unimpressed, declares that Gulliver's people must be 'the most pernicious race of little odious vermin that Nature ever suffered to crawl upon the surface of the earth' (p. 173).

---

## II.7 – England vs Brobdingnag

● Gulliver explains why the King was unimpressed.

● He discusses the values of Brobdingnag.

Look at the way Gulliver proudly portrays England in this sequence. Also note the contradiction in this chapter between Gulliver's declaration of 'an extreme love of truth' and his admission that his account has been made more favourable than 'the strictness of truth would allow' (p. 173).

Gulliver gives us reasons why he has been unable to create a good impression of England; he blames the constant questions of 'that mighty monarch' (p. 173), the King. He makes allowances for the King's narrow-mindedness because he lives 'wholly secluded from the rest of the world' (p. 174).

### Education and customs

The people of Brobdingnag only learn:

- Morality

- History

- Poetry

- The more practical forms of Mathematics

Philosophy and abstract ideas are not valued. Gulliver reads from a book to learn more about the way of life in Brobdingnag. The laws there are brief, and a well-disciplined 'army' is described in detail. There are apparently no enemies; earlier civil wars have been concluded by mutual agreement. The overall effect is of a Utopian society.

> **CHECKPOINT 17**
>
> In what ways is the book that Gulliver reads different from those he was used to?

Gulliver tries to please the King by telling him the secret of gunpowder, but the King is 'struck with horror' (p. 175) to learn that it is used to destroy nations. The King's philosophy is that 'whoever could make two ears of corn, or two blades of grass to grow upon a spot of ground where only one grew before, would deserve better of mankind' (p. 176). This is the simple adage which is the central focus of this government's rule.

Note the attack Swift makes on human weaknesses, being two-faced and behaving improperly. Swift uses this chapter to further condemn hypocrisy and political corruption.

### II.8 – Second homecoming

1. Gulliver longs to return to England.
2. An eagle picks him up and carries him until an English ship rescues him.
3. Gulliver recounts his story to the captain.
4. Gulliver returns to his family.

After two years in Brobdingnag, Gulliver longs to return home and to live his life on a normal scale. The King would like to find a woman so he might use Gulliver for breeding. Gulliver says 'I should rather have died' (p. 180). Compare this with his earlier wish to take away a dozen tiny Lilliputians for breeding (I.8).

**DID YOU KNOW?**

Gulliver appears to have travelled three hundred miles in two hours!

Glumdalclitch is unwell and they visit the sea. A trusted page looks after Gulliver here; he takes Gulliver's box further along the beach but then falls asleep. An eagle swoops down, picks the box up and then drops it and Gulliver into the sea. The box floats the right side up, but Gulliver spends an awful four hours in the water. Eventually he attracts attention by flying a distress flag and is taken aboard an English vessel. The captain, Thomas Wilcocks of Shropshire, is a little suspicious of Gulliver's appearance and manner and Gulliver insists on telling the captain his story and on showing him the evidence, which includes 'Four wasp stings, like joiners' tacks; some combings of the Queen's hair, a gold ring ...' (p. 188). The captain takes Gulliver to shore and lends him five shillings for his fare home.

Gulliver's adjustment to size when he returns home is presented in a humorous way: 'I began to think myself in Lilliput' (p. 191). Gulliver fears he will trample on other travellers and sees his friends as 'pygmies' (p. 191). At the same time, his confusion makes the tale seem more realistic.

CHECKPOINT 18

What does Gulliver find strange on his return home from Brobdingnag?

Now take a break!

## ABOUT WHOM?

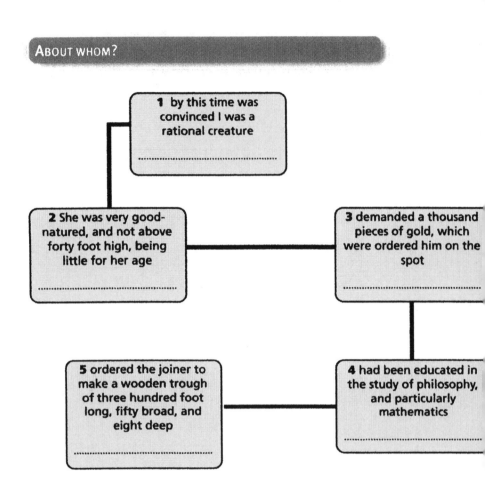

**1** by this time was convinced I was a rational creature

..................................................

**2** She was very good-natured, and not above forty foot high, being little for her age

..................................................

**3** demanded a thousand pieces of gold, which were ordered him on the spot

..................................................

**5** ordered the joiner to make a wooden trough of three hundred foot long, fifty broad, and eight deep

..................................................

**4** had been educated in the study of philosophy, and particularly mathematics

..................................................

Check your answers on p. 95.

## III.1 – The voyage of the *Hope-well*

1. Gulliver becomes surgeon on the Hope-well and they set sail.
2. Gulliver is put in charge of a sloop, which is captured by pirates.
3. He is put in a canoe and comes to an island.
4. He sees the island of Laputa in the sky and he is pulled up to it.

Captain William Robinson employs Gulliver to be ship's surgeon on the *Hope-well*. They set sail on 5 August 1706 for the East Indies. During a delay at Tonquin, Gulliver takes out a sloop, which is boarded by pirates. There is then some discussion between the Dutch officer and Japanese captain. Note their differing treatment of Gulliver: this reflects Swift's own negative attitude towards the Dutch. Gulliver's crew is taken captive by the pirate ships and Gulliver himself is 'set adrift, in a small canoe' (p. 197).

On the fifth day, Gulliver beaches the canoe at a remote island. As he walks along in the heat of the sun he suddenly finds himself in shadow. The sun has been eclipsed by 'a vast opaque body' (p. 198). He looks up to see it is a huge flying 'island in the air' (p. 199); he attracts the inhabitants' attention by waving and bowing and is pulled aboard.

> **CHECKPOINT 19**
>
> Notice the reference to 'supplicating postures' (p. 200). Where else has Gulliver behaved like this?

## III.2 – The floating island of Laputa

1. We meet the inhabitants of Laputa.

The people on the flying island of Laputa are the strangest we have yet met. They carry their heads on one side and their eyes look in different directions.

All the inhabitants are attended by '*flappers*', who smack their masters in order to attract their attention; a blow to the mouth encourages speech whereas a blow to the ears indicates they should

**DID YOU KNOW?**

The Laputans' fears that a comet would destroy the Earth, or that the Earth would fall into the sun, or that the sun would lose its energy were all actual fears of astronomers in the eighteenth century.

listen. These people are besotted with 'judicial astrology' (p. 206) and music, and their clothes bear musical and astrological symbols.

The King orders the court to entertain its inhabitants with 'the music of the spheres' (p. 204), which is a noisy and unmelodious performance. From below, the island hauls up petitions from the discontented mainland, but little is actually addressed as all ideas are expressed in either mathematical or musical terms.

### Intellectual differences

Note how we have moved from the physical differences of the miniature and gigantic into differences of intellect and understanding. These people are not practical and are unable to think logically. We are given several examples of this, such as the defective buildings and that Gulliver's new clothes fail to fit. Gulliver claims the inhabitants have a complete lack of imagination.

In this world, Swift cynically portrays the clever and top level of society to be disassociated from reality. The less intelligent people are actually more practical, and more capable of running the island.

The women of this island are left to their own devices as the men are simply obsessed by the possible destruction of the island. The women are kept in luxury and idleness on the island and are visited by admirers from the mainland below.

**CHECKPOINT 20**

Compare the role of women here and in Lilliput.

## III.3 – Magnetism and rule

1. Gulliver explains Laputa's propulsion system.
2. We hear how the King maintains rule over Balnibari.

Gulliver tells us in detail about the island's magnetic system and propulsion. He also describes how the King of Laputa controls the people on Balnibarbi – the land that lies beneath the floating island. He does so by obscuring the sun and rain, or even by landing the island on them. The cities defend themselves by hiding under natural rocks or by being protected by massive towers specially built for the purpose. Note the cynical view expressed by Swift in this chapter, of the relationship between the governed and the governors.

**CHECKPOINT 21**

Gulliver appears to be measuring again. Why is this important?

## III.4 – The poverty of Balnibari

1. Gulliver goes to Balnibari.
2. Balnibari is very poor in comparison with Laputa.
3. Gulliver visits the Academy of Projectors.

Gulliver asks for permission to visit Balnibarbi where he finds extreme poverty and distress. The people are 'generally in rags' (p. 219) and look desolate and miserable. Gulliver stays with Lord Munodi where he finds just the opposite; notice the contrast between Munodi's palace and the land outside. Lord Munodi's estate is well kept and orderly but the people hate Munodi himself. Up above on the island, new rules for running Balnibarbi have been

**GLOSSARY**

**judicial astrology** fortune telling using the position of the stars

**the music of the spheres** the planets were once believed to create music as they moved, but this sound was inaudible to the human ear

passed, to modernise their lifestyles; meanwhile below 'the whole country lies miserably waste, the houses in ruins, and the people without food or clothes' (p. 222).

## The poverty problem

This chapter parodies eighteenth-century Ireland where the poor starved whilst the economists argued over political reforms. Swift wrote *A Modest Proposal* (1729) as a direct parody of this chapter.

Gulliver visits the main 'Academy of Projectors' (p. 221) and finds even more bizarre practices; poor design and faulty structures are replacing effective and working buildings. Munodi has taken on one of these to replace a good working mill on his estate.

### III.5 – The Academy of Lagado

&#9312; Gulliver visits the Academy of Lagado.

&#9313; The bizarre research that takes place there is described.

Gulliver visits the Academy of Lagado, where the academics in some five hundred rooms do the most extraordinary research:

- The extraction of sunlight from cucumbers

- Making pillows from marble

- Abolishing words and replacing them with actions in the language

- Turning ice to gunpowder

- The mixing of paint by a blind man

- Building a house by starting with the roof

- A new form of ploughing by letting pigs roam free

- The joining of a sundial to a weathercock to link sunshine with wind

- Curing colic by using a pair of bellows

In the department of speculative learning Gulliver watches a word machine being operated. In the school of languages three professors reduce all words to monosyllables and eliminate all verbs. In the mathematical school propositions are literally swallowed by writing them on wafers which are eaten!

Note Jonathan Swift's tongue-in-cheek condemnation of academics. Many of these bizarre examples were based on actual papers produced by the Royal Society, so once again Jonathan Swift uses satire.

**DID YOU KNOW?**

Computers have been used in recent years to produce random selections of words and music, rather like the process Swift is mocking here!

## III.6 – More about the Academy

1 **Sensible ideas are considered abnormal.**

2 **Gulliver suggests some ideas for improvements.**

This is simply a further account of the Academy. We are told that the professors seem to be 'wholly out of their senses' (p. 232). Here

**CHECKPOINT 22**

What were coloured silks produced from?

**DID YOU KNOW?**
The Academy satirises the philosophical emphasis on rational thought that was prevalent in the seventeenth and eighteenth centuries.

sensible ideas are treated as abnormal. There is an inversion of the satirical elements. A doctor has devised physical ways of bringing about improved government by shortening debates, prompt action by ministers and an insistence that members vote in an opposite direction to the views they have expressed. The most peculiar 'clue' is to surgically fuse two halves of brains that hold opposite opinions, therefore bringing about political reconciliation. Taxes are levied – after neighbours assess each other's vices, or after people assess their own virtues. The schemes of government proposed here are 'wild impossible chimeras' (p. 232). Compare this with the disease-ridden administration.

Gulliver assists one professor by contributing the idea that men could be taken away and their letters and papers searched for evidence of spying. This is a direct reference to 'the Kingdom of Tribnia (Britain), by the natives called Langden (England)' (p. 236).

### III.7 – Gulliver visits Glubbdubdrib

**①** Gulliver sails to Glubbdubdrib.

**②** Gulliver encounters a number of ghosts.

Gulliver sets sail for Maldonada, hoping to travel on a ship from there to Luggnagg. However, as this is not possible, he sails to Glubbdubdrib instead, the 'Island of *Sorcerers* or *Magicians*', which lies fifteen miles to the south-west. The dead are called up to serve the governor for twenty-four hours; this makes Gulliver's 'flesh creep with a horror' (p. 239). The grisly spectacle of ghosts is the hardest scene we have witnessed so far. Gulliver is allowed to call up the ghosts of 'whatever persons I would choose to name' (p. 240). Among many others, Gulliver chooses to see the ghosts of:

- Alexander, who discloses to Gulliver that the real reason for his death was that he was drunk

- Hannibal crossing the Alps

**DID YOU KNOW?**
It is no accident that Swift brings the ancients into this chapter. He also favours them in his *Battle of the Books.*

- Caesar and Pompey, ready to fight each other
- The Senate of Rome, which faces a modern parliament
- Brutus, who is described with admiration

Caesar tells Gulliver about the '*sextumvirate*' in the afterlife – an exclusive group of the ex-leaders 'to which all the ages of the world cannot add a seventh' (p. 241).

Note how this story actually links with the real world of Jonathan Swift (see **Setting and background**).

## III.8 – A ghostly history lesson

① Gulliver calls up more ghosts.

② He learns the 'true' version of historical events.

Gulliver calls up **Homer** and **Aristotle**, who are attended by hosts of ignorant commentators who declare they are now ashamed of their criticisms of these great ancients. Homer finds that two of his critics lack poetic appreciation. Aristotle accuses his of being stupid.

He then meets **Descartes** and **Gassendi**, and they discuss philosophy with Aristotle. Aristotle is undeterred by the new movements in philosophical thinking, declaring that the new systems would soon be 'out of vogue' (p. 243).

Turning his attention to the 'modern dead' (p. 243), Gulliver is disappointed when he explores the ancestry of noble families. He finds the lineage interrupted by 'pages, lackeys, valets' (p. 244), and is disgusted to find that many great men have acquired their greatness and wealth by engaging in 'sodomy or incest' (p.245), prostitution and poisoning.

**CHECKPOINT 23**

Who are the exclusive group of six?

**CHECKPOINT 24**

Two villagers and a courtier are deliberately placed together here. Why do you think this is?

**GLOSSARY**

**chimeras** fantasies

**Alexander the Great** died in 324BC after defeating Darius of Persia in 331BC

**Hannibal** Carthaginian general who took 60,000 men and crossed the Alps on elephants to invade Italy

**Caesar and Pompey** two famous Roman leaders

**Brutus** committed suicide after murdering Caesar

**Homer** Greek poet of (probably) the eighth century BC

**Aristotle** Greek philosopher (384-322 BC)

**Descartes and Gassendi** two French philosophers of the seventeenth century

**DID YOU KNOW?**

The dismissal of the theory of 'attraction' (p. 243) actually refers to Newton's modern theory of gravity.

## Criticism of European culture

Note how this passage comments on every kind of vice and injustice. This is Swift's most damning comment on Europe past and present.

**DID YOU KNOW?**

Japan did not allow any Europeans to enter the country at that time, except for the Dutch.

### III.9 – Licking the royal dust

**1** Gulliver sails to Luggnagg.

**2** The King receives him.

Gulliver sets sail on a one-month voyage to Luggnagg. He tells his story to an official on arrival and is then confined for two weeks. Note how Gulliver, who is now travelling to Japan, has assumed the identity of 'a Hollander' (p. 248).

Finally Gulliver receives royal permission to visit the King to '*lick the dust before his footstool*' (p. 249). This is a very literal function and leaves an unwelcome petitioner with a mouth full of dust, which ensures they cannot speak when they eventually see the King

The King disposes of his enemies by poisoning the dust. However, the floor is cleaned for Gulliver; he is received well by the King and stays for three months.

## III.10 – The Stuldbruggs

❶ Gulliver praises the Luggnaggians

❷ The Stuldbruggs are described.

❸ Gulliver is horrified when he meets them.

### Immortality

Gulliver learns from a Luggnaggian about a race of immortals known as Struldbruggs or Immortals. Gulliver is filled with 'inexpressible delight' (p. 252) by the idea of immortality. He has good intentions of using his meeting with the Struldbruggs to stop the progressive corruption of the human race, and is happy to be able to speak to them. This joy quickly turns to horror as he finds them to be 'not only opinionative, peevish, covetous, morose, vain, talkative, but incapable of friendship, and dead to all natural affection' (p. 257). This has affected the Luggnaggians considerably; they now have no desire to go on living, as all they can look forward to is an endless old age. This is described as a 'dreadful prospect' (p. 257).

This passage could be interpreted as a sermon by Swift to help people come to terms with death and welcome the Christian prospect of a life after death.

---

**CHECKPOINT 24**

Compare Gulliver's judgement 'dreadful prospect' with his previous ideas on immortality.

---

**? DID YOU KNOW?**

This episode is reminiscent of the classical myth of Tithonus. Eos, the goddess of dawn, asked the gods to grant her lover immortality but forgot to ask for eternal youth.

## III.11 – The third homecoming

1 **Gulliver is offered a job but refuses it.**

2 **Gulliver sails back to Japan.**

3 **From there he sails to England, via Amsterdam.**

Gulliver refuses a job, the first he has been offered on his travels, by the King of Luggnagg and sets sail for Japan on 6 May 1709. When he arrives at Nangasac he takes a job as a ship's surgeon on a Dutch ship bound for Amsterdam. Gulliver works hard to pass himself off as a Dutchman and claims to have relatives in Holland. He is still pretending to be a Dutchman, for his own safety. He travels from Amsterdam back home after an absence of five years and six months. At Redriff he finds 'my wife and family in good health' (p. 263).

**CHECKPOINT 26**

Are you satisfied with the description of Gulliver's homecoming?

Now take a break!

## ABOUT WHOM/WHAT?

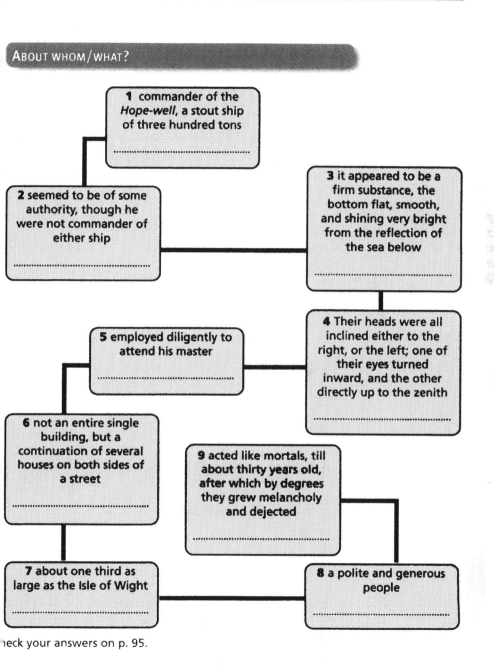

**1** commander of the *Hope-well*, a stout ship of three hundred tons

.............................................

**2** seemed to be of some authority, though he were not commander of either ship

.............................................

**3** it appeared to be a firm substance, the bottom flat, smooth, and shining very bright from the reflection of the sea below

.............................................

**4** Their heads were all inclined either to the right, or the left; one of their eyes turned inward, and the other directly up to the zenith

.............................................

**5** employed diligently to attend his master

.............................................

**6** not an entire single building, but a continuation of several houses on both sides of a street

.............................................

**9** acted like mortals, till about thirty years old, after which by degrees they grew melancholy and dejected

.............................................

**7** about one third as large as the Isle of Wight

.............................................

**8** a polite and generous people

.............................................

heck your answers on p. 95.

## IV.1 – Houyhnhnms and Yahoos

**1** Gulliver has a difficult voyage to the South Seas.

**2** He is marooned on a strange land.

**3** He encounters the Yahoos and the Houyhnhnms.

> **CHECKPOINT 27**
>
> What is Gulliver's state of mind immediately before the mutiny?

On 7 September 1710 Gulliver sets sail from Portsmouth, as captain of the *Adventure* to the South Seas via the West Indies. Sickness strikes the ship and some of the crew are lost. Those crew members are replaced in the West Indies by buccaneers in disguise. These men quickly corrupt the rest of the crew and mutiny. Gulliver is confined to his cabin for weeks and then marooned in an unknown country.

He comes across a group of 'ugly monsters' (p. 270) that are prepared to attack him like savages, but he is rescued when they run away at the sight of a horse. The horse inspects him and then discusses him with another horse! Gulliver decides they must be magicians in disguise and makes a polite speech to them. They teach Gulliver two words: '*Yahoo*' and '*Houyhnhnm*' (p. 273), and then Gulliver is signalled by the grey horse to go with him. Note that the ugly creatures have human form and the creatures with human characteristics are horses.

> **CHECKPOINT 28**
>
> Why do you think Gulliver's speech is comic?

## IV.2 – Among the Yahoos

**1** The horses take Gulliver to a stable.

**2** Gulliver is compared with the Yahoos.

Gulliver goes with the horses and is led to a stable. Gulliver still expects to meet the human owners of these horses and eventually realises that this is not to be the case. The grey horse introduces Gulliver to a mare and foal and then puts Gulliver next to a Yahoo so that he may be compared to them. Gulliver is relieved that he wears clothes which helps to distinguish him from 'this abominable animal, a perfect human figure; the face of it indeed was flat and broad, the nose depressed, the lips large, and the mouth wide' (p. 276).

**CHECK THE NET**
If you search for 'Gulliver' the most popular results are for travel agencies!

Gulliver is unable to eat either the ass-meat offered to the Yahoo or the oats the Houyhnhnms eat. Gulliver accepts a bowl of milk and makes himself some porridge. A sledge drawn by four Yahoos brings an elderly horse to dine. Gulliver sleeps on a bed of straw between the house of the Houyhnhnms and the stable of the Yahoos.

## IV.3 – At home with the Houyhnhnms

1 Gulliver learns how to communicate with the Houyhnhnms.

2 Gulliver describes his journey.

3 Gulliver is compared to a Yahoo.

Gulliver and 'master' (p. 280) communicate and Gulliver learns the language by imitating the nasal sounds expressed by the horse. The grey horse is obsessed with observing the differences between Gulliver and the Yahoos; he is 'extremely curious to know from what part of the country I came' (p. 281). Gulliver is seen as a separate species due mainly to his clothes. However one morning the sorrel nag, Gulliver's valet, sees him undressed and goes to tell his master. Gulliver demonstrates how he is able to take off and put on his clothes. Fortunately the grey horse seems to be more interested with Gulliver's intellect than his physical deficiencies.

**CHECKPOINT 29**

What is meant by 'appearances of reason'?

Gulliver gives the grey horse an account of how he came to be there but the horse thinks that he is telling lies, as he puts it, saying *'the thing which was not'* (p. 281). The horse cannot comprehend another country being beyond the sea, or that the sea may be travelled in boats made by creatures like the Yahoos. Although he sees the physical likeness with the Yahoos, he is prepared to ignore it for the meantime.

At the end of the chapter the Houyhnhnms conclude that without clothes and except for his preference for walking on his hind legs, Gulliver would be a Yahoo. Swift identifies only two differences between humans and animals:

1. Men wear clothes

2. Men write their thoughts on paper

**?** **DID YOU KNOW?**

Gulliver compares the horse speech to German. This is thought to be a reference to Emperor Charles V (1500–58), who is reported to have said that he would 'address his God in Spanish, his mistress in Italian, and his horse in German'.

## IV.4 – Horses, humans and Houyhnhnms

1. Gulliver describes horses to the Houyhnhnms.

2. He then tells them about Europe and England.

What Gulliver tells his 'master' is incomprehensible to him. Gulliver explains that horses in England are groomed and cared for by Yahoos. Unfortunately, Gulliver goes on to explain spurs and castration, and his own embarrassment at the grey's 'noble resentment at our savage treatment of the Houyhnhnms' (p. 288) is obvious. Swift uses Gulliver to display embarrassment at the treatment of horses at home, when it parallels exactly the Houyhnhnm treatment of the Yahoos.

Gulliver tries for a third time to explain his background and his journey but finds difficulty in explaining why some of his crew have been punished and banished. It takes several days to explain this, but eventually the Houyhnhnm seems to be able to distinguish the human race. Swift then develops the line of inquiry from Gulliver to more general issues and then to European society.

**CHECKPOINT 30**

What reactions does the the Houyhnhnm master have to what Gulliver has to say?

## IV.5 – War and law

① Gulliver explains war.

② Gulliver explains law.

In the next two paragraphs Gulliver explains the causes of war and therefore human history at its worst. Gulliver talks about England in particular and lists the causes of war and how the soldier is really just a trained killer. The grey horse cannot understand how the European is so strong when man is obviously physically inferior. This leads Gulliver into a detailed account of warlike operations and strategies, but the grey is unimpressed and concludes that these people (Europeans) must be more corrupted than the naturally vicious Yahoos.

**CHECKPOINT 31**

Why does the master think that humans are more corrupt than Yahoos?

### Gulliver's view of English law

Note the detailed description Gulliver gives of the legal system in England, and how lawyers are trained to prove the opposite of truth in courts of law.

Note too the English use of precedents, where what has gone before will always be used as a yardstick. In the cases where injustice has prevailed, the worst of errors are thereby perpetuated.

Look at the use of legal terms to confuse the ordinary person.

Consider Gulliver's assertion that lawyers are generally the most ignorant and prejudiced professionals.

Gulliver gives a very black and white account of the legal profession, explaining that English law is based on precedent, which makes certain that whatever has been done in the past may be done again and that the lawyers 'take special care to record all the decisions formerly made against common justice' (p. 296).

## IV.6 – English society

① Gulliver describes money.

② Gulliver explains disease.

③ Gulliver explains the term 'Minister of State'.

This is Jonathan Swift's most scathing attack on English society and gives us an insight into '*the state of England*' under Queen Anne (p. 298).

In this chapter Gulliver tries to describe money, how it is minted, and how it is used. He describes the difference in wealth: 'the bulk of our people was forced to live miserably, by labouring every day for small wages to make a few live plentifully' (p. 298). He claims that man's needs are more luxurious and this leads to degeneration, 'diseases, folly and vice' (p. 299). Note the contrast that Gulliver portrays between the desperate corruption in England and that of the lifestyle of the depraved Yahoos. The Houyhnhnms cannot understand disease, and when Gulliver explains ill health he includes an attack on his own profession, and gives examples of unprofessional practice.

> **CHECKPOINT 32**
>
> How many of incidents of unprofessional practice can you remember?

The Houyhnhnms ask Gulliver to explain the expression 'Minister of State'. The chapter concludes with Gulliver's scathing account of ministerial functions, and even more derisory remarks on the nobility. Note the exaggeration of all Gulliver's examples.

## IV.7 – Human nature

**Gulliver and the master compare humans with Yahoos.**

Gulliver explains why he has portrayed England and the English in such a dreadful way; he feels he has found faults within himself. Gulliver also feels a loyalty towards the Houyhnhnms which has resolved him not to return home but to stay in this land of honesty and virtue.

The grey reflects upon the English. He declares they must have limited intellect, which they use to increase corruption. The grey concludes from Gulliver's similarity to the Yahoos that there is an intellectual similarity also. He now sees the Yahoos as quarrelsome, selfish and greedy; these are all similar vices to those expressed by Gulliver. Gulliver portrays the human race as a **people** who are intelligent but overindulgent and wicked.

### Comparisons

The master goes on to describe the way in which the Yahoos collect shiny pebbles and jealously guard them, causing tribal wars. Note the direct comparison between shiny pebbles and diamonds. This is Swift's **satirical** comment on avarice, jealousy and greed – all human vices for the reader to reflect on.

The Yahoos eat anything they can steal, and after they have overeaten they need laxatives; nearly all the ill health they experience is due to overeating.

The grey goes on to describe sexual promiscuity and dirtiness among the Yahoos, and how hard work cures an attack of low spirits.

The master portrays the Yahoos as cunning and savage animals who **ironically** demonstrate the same vices as humans.

 **DID YOU KNOW?**
Gluttony is one of the seven deadly sins. Can you spot any of the others in *Gulliver's Travels*?

## IV.8 – Bath attack!

1. **A female Yahoo accosts Gulliver when he is bathing.**

2. **Gulliver describes the lifestyle of the Houyhnhnms.**

Gulliver is determined to take a closer look at the Yahoos, hoping to make comparisons to prove the horses wrong. As he is bathing, a young Yahoo female accosts him and this gives the horses even more proof that he is indeed a Yahoo. Interestingly, Gulliver seems to have enjoyed the encounter: he describes her as not 'altogether so hideous' as the others and that she 'stood gazing and howling all the time I was putting on my clothes' (p. 315).

Gulliver turns his attention to the Houyhnhnms, who seem to have no differences of opinion, which means they have no need for book learning or philosophy, and, as we learn at the end of the chapter, their national parliament only needs to meet every four years to share oats, Yahoos, cows and so on equally amongst themselves.

The Houyhnhnms offer friendship and benevolence in all their relationships; their offspring are brought up without close emotional attachments. Marriages are carefully arranged, without a wedding ceremony, but also with domestic disputes! The young

**DID YOU KNOW?**
Gulliver's observations that redheaded Yahoos are 'more libidinous and mischievous' is a reference to Swift's admirer, the Duchess of Somerset, who was nicknamed 'Carrots'.

**DID YOU KNOW?**
This chapter is equally divided between the Yahoos and the Houyhnhnms. Gulliver appears superior to the Yahoos, but inferior to the Houyhnhnms.

horses are treated equally irrespective of their sex, their grazing is controlled and exercise is encouraged. The competitive sports are rather Spartan in their characteristics.

## IV.9 – A council meeting

① **A council meeting discusses the Yahoos.**

② **More of the Houyhnhnms' lifestyle is described.**

We are introduced to a council meeting, which is involved in the same debate as to the origin and future of the Yahoos. The master, who remembers Gulliver's story of castrating horses, suggests that the young Yahoos should be gelded. Note that the horses use the Yahoos for haulage, just as we use horses.

### An alternative view of culture

The Houyhnhnms have no need of books, their past is simply remembered, and they have no need of medicine, as their wounds need little attention. Poetry is also limited. Swift himself had a passion for writing, history and poetry. These are denounced in this chapter, as the perfect world of the Houyhnhnms does not study these topics.

Their study of astronomy is limited to the sun and the moon. The Houyhnhnms build houses that are made of wattle and well constructed and carry their tools in their fetlocks. They are not frightened or apprehensive about dying; they visit their friends to say goodbye prior to their death. The only negative word in their language is 'Yahoo'.

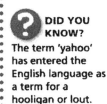 **DID YOU KNOW?**
The term 'yahoo' has entered the English language as a term for a hooligan or lout.

## IV.10 – Time to go home

1. Gulliver feels settled.

2. The Council decides that Gulliver must leave.

3. Gulliver bids farewell to the Houyhnhnms.

Gulliver has settled into a simple life. He has made chairs, clothes and found simple foods very enjoyable, especially honey. Gulliver is frequently in his master's company, where he learns to hate his own race. He now looks on his own kind as 'Yahoos in shape and disposition' (p. 327). He even goes as far as to adopt some horse-like habits: he trots and neighs. Note the very drastic contrasts in this chapter between the virtuous Houyhnhnms and the savage Yahoos.

The Council of the Houyhnhnms has decided that Gulliver must leave and the grey horse has reluctantly agreed that Gulliver must leave also. There are fears that if he stays he will organise the Yahoos into some kind of mutiny. Gulliver is shocked by the news, interpreting it as nothing more than a death sentence. He tells the Houyhnhnms that if he does survive, he will be destined to live a contemptible life.

> **CHECKPOINT 33**
>
> What does Gulliver promise to do when he gets home?

The devoted sorrel nag and Gulliver build a canoe out of wattle and Yahoo skins; it has a sail and paddles. The Yahoos help Gulliver take it to the beach. A tearful farewell concludes this chapter. Gulliver is allowed to kiss his master's hoof. Note the extraordinary mark of distinction in Gulliver being allowed to kiss the horse's hoof, and the use of Yahoo skins as hide to cover the canoe. Aren't these the wrong way round?

## IV.11 – The final homecoming

**1** Gulliver is taken aboard a ship.

**2** Gulliver returns home.

**3** He prefers the company of horses to people.

As Gulliver leaves he hopes to find a deserted island where he can live without corruption. He is sailing in the direction of Western Australia; he finds a rocky inlet and beaches the canoe there. Naked savages occupy the island. After only three days a landing party takes him aboard a Portuguese vessel. The sailors realise he is European by the colour of his skin but are confused by his strange dress and question him. The captain of the ship, Don Pedro de Mendez, is 'a very courteous and generous person' (p. 335). The Portuguese Captain is probably the nicest character in the book. He takes considerable time and patience to understand Gulliver.

Gulliver perceives the crew as Yahoos and attempts to jump overboard. The Captain takes him to Lisbon and then home to his wife and family. We are told the sight of his family fills him with 'hatred, disgust and contempt' (p. 338). Gulliver is unable to touch any of his family and ensures they do not use his supper plate. He buys two young horses and he spends four hours each day talking to them. Gulliver now prefers the company of his horses or his groom to that of his wife.

> **CHECKPOINT 34**
>
> How effective is the Captain's attempt to rehabilitate Gulliver?

## IV.12 – A final few words

① Gulliver asserts the truth of his story.

The reader wants to learn more of Gulliver and his family; instead we are only asked to believe in the author's honesty. Swift concludes his novel by testifying that *Gulliver's Travels* are the truth and not a fiction to amuse. Gulliver says 'I rather chose to relate plain matter of fact in the simplest manner and style, because my principal design was to inform, and not to amuse thee' (p. 340). He goes on to say he has written without a view to making money, quite simply to inform the public.

Gulliver feels the Brobdingnagians are the least corrupted of the Yahoos; he then goes on to discuss the possible colonisation of these countries. The encounter with the Houyhnhnms has left Gulliver with a sympathy for horses.

Gulliver contrasts the tyrannical European colonies with a beneficial invasion of Houyhnhnms. He continues to give the reader a résumé of Houyhnhnm features in Yahoo surroundings.

> **A final view of Gulliver**
>
> Swift finishes the book by giving the reader insight into Gulliver. We are left with a picture of pride, vanity and misanthropy to such a huge degree that it becomes almost comic; the character is now unrealistic.

**? DID YOU KNOW?**
Did you know? The quotation from Virgil's *Aeneid* that 'fortune has made him wretched, but has not made him a liar' is ironical because in the *Aeneid* the assertion follows a lie about the Trojan Horse. Does this mean that Jonathan Swift with tongue in cheek is declaring loudly that Gulliver's story is indeed a work of fiction?

Now take a break!

## ABOUT WHOM?

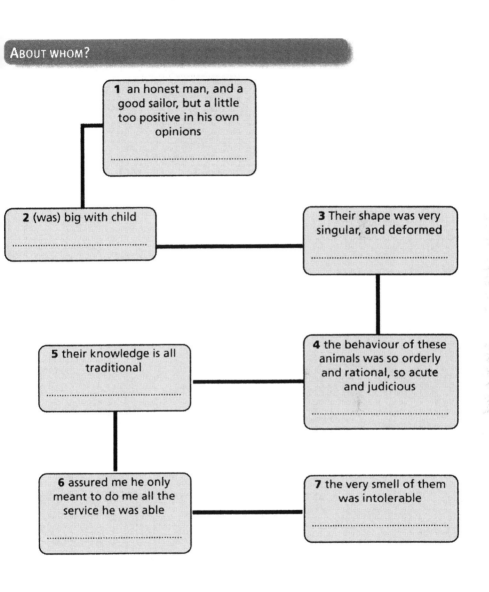

**1** an honest man, and a good sailor, but a little too positive in his own opinions

...................................

**2** (was) big with child

...................................

**3** Their shape was very singular, and deformed

...................................

**5** their knowledge is all traditional

...................................

**4** the behaviour of these animals was so orderly and rational, so acute and judicious

...................................

**6** assured me he only meant to do me all the service he was able

...................................

**7** the very smell of them was intolerable

...................................

Check your answers on p. 95.

## PART THREE

## COMMENTARY

# THEMES

## POLITICAL REFERENCES

Some parallels may be drawn between *Gulliver's Travels* and the politicians and political events of the times. The table opposite may help us to better understand some of the characters, events and opinions represented.

## SATIRE

**DID YOU KNOW?**

The early eighteenth century, when *Gulliver's Travels* was written, has been called the golden age of satire.

**DID YOU KNOW?**

The Romans established satire as a literary form.

Frequently at this time literature was used as a political tool. It was used to send messages, make people think, and to make subversive criticism of monarchy, political parties, or religious factions. To do this effectively the author used **satire**. This is where writing exposes the follies of human behaviour by presenting it as absurd or ridiculous. It is not what is said that is important but what is inferred.

The whole of *Gulliver's Travels* is **ironical**. The Englishman in the strange land surrounded by miniature beings is no more than an outsider. In the first Part we see ourselves as one of these miniature beings. In the second Part Gulliver is overwhelmingly human, with human weaknesses, e.g. distorting the truth, and human strengths, e.g. the positive oration. In the last Part the situational satire moves beyond our feeling comfortable with it. In this Part there is a complete transposition of horse and man. We see a civilisation that is pure and rational. It has not been influenced by fraud, deceit, illness or greed.

Swift writes of all sorts of social injustices and personal discomfort. Often the writing contains biting sarcasm but sometimes there are violent explosions of anger, and quiet ridicule is frequent. However he achieves his satire, the intention is the same and he urges the reader to really think about the effect of these views.

| | |
|---|---|
| George I | Similar to the Emperor of Lilliput – both enjoyed music and military parades |
| Walpole | Was once helped by the Duchess of Kendal to return to power; could be Flimnap, the Treasurer, who was saved by one of the King's cushions |
| Walpole's wife | Said to be unfaithful – could be likened to the wife of the Prime Minister of Laputa |
| Whigs | A political party referred to as Slamecksan in the novel |
| Tories | A political party referred to as Tramecksan in the novel |
| Catholics | Referred to as Big-Endians in the novel |
| Protestants | Referred to as Little-Endians in the novel |
| The Whig Committee of Secrecy 1715, which inquired into the Treaty of Utrecht | Could be compared with the Articles of Impeachment against Quinbus Flestrin |
| The Order of the Garter, the Bath and the Thistle, all orders of merit in Jonathan Swift's time | Referred to as 'coloured threads' in the novel |
| English oppression of Ireland | Could be reflected in the oppressive behaviour of Laputa to Balnibarbi |
| Absentee landlords in Ireland, actually living in England | Could be compared to Ministers' Estates in Balnibarbi |
| The failure of the Irish agricultural system | Referred to as 'soil so unhappily cultivated' (p. 219) |
| Halley's Comet, 1682 – a spectacular sight, said to be an omen | Referred to as 'the last comet' (p. 206) |
| The Royal Society – frequently ridiculed by cynics | Like the Academy of Projectors |

Swift intends that even the most far-fetched of his characters is meant to remind the reader of human weaknesses; we are asked to consider lust, barbarism, pride and conceit. Often Swift gives us direct comparisons. Two good examples of these are the people in the court at Lilliput and their antics to procure promotion, and the people in the Academy at Lagado and their time-consuming and worthless research.

As we travel through each Part the humanity becomes more degenerate and despicable and we are left to face ourselves in the Yahoos, whereas the well-bred horse portrays the superior, sensitive, intelligent and virtuous characteristics.

### Lilliput

In the world of Lilliput we view with some amusement how meaningless the lives at court are. The ceremonies become silly, the awarding of honours meaningless, and the political differences completely comic when we consider that such rivalry is over which end an egg is eaten from! The whole 'seriousness' of Lilliput is reduced to merely a sideshow where we, the spectators, see the action for what it really is: nonsense.

### Brobdingnag

An alternative environment at Brobdingnag suggests a complete contrast with Lilliput and we see things from exactly the opposite perspective. The close-up pictures of skin, nipple and food repulse the reader and we are left to question how we judge beauty and elegance. Other people become physically unattractive to Gulliver in Brobdingnag, just as he himself became socially and intellectually unattractive in Lilliput. In the former the characters are ridiculed, in the latter it is society as a whole that is held up to ridicule.

Ironically, now Gulliver is twelve times smaller, it is his people who are ridiculed by the King of Brobdingnag – just as he, Gulliver, has ridiculed the antics of the Lilliputians.

**? DID YOU KNOW?**
Swift invented the name Lilliput, but now the word 'lilliputian' may be applied to anyone of diminutive size, since *Gulliver's Travels* has become so well known.

## Size

Parts I and II reverse the perspectives completely. Gulliver is a 'Brobdingnagian' in Lilliput. Here among miniature men he witnesses their spite and envy. Contrary to this, Gulliver is a 'Lilliputian' in Brobdingnag and witnesses, despite his fears, the generosity and benevolence of the giants. Indeed it is only in this Part that Gulliver holds a tender relationship – with Glumdalclitch, in an 'Alice in Wonderland' kind of way.

The use of the sizing up and down by a factor of twelve demonstrates the inconsequence of size and focuses us back to the fact that we are what we believe, not how we live in physical terms. We see that wisdom, integrity, honesty and loyalty are independent of size.

## *Laputa*

In Part III Swift turns his attention to virtues (or lack of them). The focus of Laputa is intellectual and cognitive. In Part III we need to consider four main areas of satire. Swift attacks the false learning and bizarre research by making the projectors eccentric and obsessive. He uses the oppression of Balnibarbi by Laputa to remind the reader of the Anglo-Irish issues. He refers to unrewarded efforts and political corruption and even the desire for eternal life by using the Struldbruggs. Throughout all of Part III the reader is forced to use his or her intellect.

## *The Houyhnhnms*

In the fourth Part, we are given a contrast awful in its extremities. The Yahoos with their human form and bestiality are contrasted with the horse-like Houyhnhnms who display virtues far above those observed in human society. The satire in this Part is aimed at the Yahoos; Swift uses them as a device to explain how awful the human race really is. The comparisons are individual and in political groups. The comparisons are frequently odious, and in some cases indecent. Swift uses all of the skills in his power to demonstrate the gross behaviour of the human being.

**DID YOU KNOW?**
*'La puta'* is Spanish for 'prostitute' and the name is almost certainly deliberate. What is being prostituted – i.e. misused – in this land?

Gulliver

# CHARACTERS

## GULLIVER

Gulliver plays a more prominent role in Parts I and II. He is treated ceremoniously and with high regard by the Lilliputians, and with affection by the Brobdingnagians, who regard him almost as an interesting pet. The high regard of the Lilliputians is not seen in Part III where the Laputans quite simply ignore him. The only interaction he has in Part III is with the academics of Lagado, and then only to demonstrate the magical understanding these people seem to have of life and logic. By Part IV Gulliver is looked upon suspiciously, almost with disgust as he is regarded as a kind of Yahoo.

### Struggle

Gulliver may be compared with Christian in *The Pilgrim's Progress* (by John Bunyan, 1684) and Robinson Crusoe in *The Life and Adventures of Robinson Crusoe* (by Daniel Defoe, 1719). Each book was written by a Puritan at about the same time. The characters were used to portray various types of struggle:

● CHRISTIAN – over salvation

● CRUSOE – over daily hardships and eventually for survival

● GULLIVER – over the political and moral problems facing government

It could be said that each of these characters becomes responsible for his own actions and adventures, each represents true honesty, and each even wins the devotion of an equally honest friend in Hopeful, Man Friday and Glumdalclitch.

### Honesty and insight

Gulliver is portrayed as an honest, educated man determined to earn a living as a ship's surgeon at sea. He is philosophical about the adventures and mishaps he encounters. He faces the new and wonderful people with genuine interest and relays details refreshingly and without malice. It is Gulliver's attention to detail

**CHECKPOINT 35**

Can Gulliver be considered a symbol of honesty?

that gives us an insight into the wonderful worlds Gulliver visits. We see, hear and experience through Gulliver's senses. This, in turn, helps us to decide very effectively about Gulliver's personality, his likes and dislikes, his joys and fears, his morality and political preferences.

## A sense of honour

Gulliver has a sense of honour; he has left his family in order to provide for them. He is reminded of his oath to the Emperor and feels embarrassed when he is publicly displayed. His respect for royalty is witnessed with his dealings with the princess. Gulliver gently kisses her hand and bends low. This is linked with his sense of patriotism; for Gulliver, England is best. When he explains to the King about England he tends to ignore the weaknesses of the English system of law and government. We know Gulliver is interested by politics, frequently holding conversations on biased appointments, irrelevant wars and dishonest elections. We also learn he has anti-militaristic views and is especially critical of people who fight simply for money. Yet despite this view we learn that Gulliver himself must have been trained to use hand sword, staff and pistols because he uses all these effectively on his journeys.

## An enquiring mind

Gulliver is above all else a good conversationalist, always ready to ask and answer questions; he has an enquiring mind and is keen to learn. This is demonstrated by:

- Learning new languages
- Ability to make accurate measurements
- Interest in history

## Gulliver's relationships

Gulliver takes easily to all spheres of society, whether it is emperor or king, tradesman or servant. He is always ready to help or give helpful advice where he thinks it will be valued.

If we have a criticism of Gulliver it is that he does not seem to have deep affection for his wife and child. We are told in Part IV 'I left

**DID YOU KNOW?**
In *A Clockwork Orange* 'gulliver' is a slang word for 'head', deriving from 'golova', Russian for 'head'.

my poor wife big with child' (p. 267) and when he returns home she
kisses him and Gulliver is appalled, 'having not been used to the
touch of that odious animal for so many years' (p. 339).

Indeed, he clearly leaves the adventures for a warm relationship
with the inhabitants of his stable. About his groom, Gulliver says, 'I
feel my spirits revived by the smell he contracts in the stable' (p. 339).

### Gulliver as a human being

Generally, Gulliver portrays each scene in a positive light, and
wishes to be perceived in the same way; an example of this is when
he displays his clemency by sparing the ruffians and is commended
for his actions at court. Gulliver has impeccable and genteel
manners, made laughable by the differences in size in both Lilliput
and Brobdingnag.

Jonathan Swift uses Gulliver as an example of a 'good' human being
but throughout the book we are continually asked to question how
good human beings really are. Gulliver horrifies the King with the
secret of gunpowder yet is horrified that promotions in Lilliput rely
on whether the applicant has gymnastic skills! In Part IV it is Yahoo
skins Gulliver uses for his canoe, not the horse skins in common use
by his civilisation.

### Gulliver as a literary device

Jonathan Swift uses Gulliver to deny accusations or to
embarrassingly embellish an argument only to give us an even
clearer understanding of the human frailties being portrayed. So the
'innocent' Gulliver is used as a catalyst to allow the reader a deeper
understanding of certain issues. An example of this is clothing,
which is all that distinguishes Gulliver from the Yahoos.

These shock tactics culminate in a graphic portrayal of the Yahoos.
Jonathan Swift makes us stop to reflect upon the unspoken natural
moments of our lives that link us more to animals than we care to
admit. Indeed most readers identify, as Gulliver did, with the
Houyhnhnms. This must be the absolute irony, as irony is
impossible in the Houyhnhnms' society because '*the thing which is*

**? DID YOU KNOW?**
Gulliver (and
therefore Swift) is
often perceived to
be a misogynist
(someone who
hates women).

---

### Shock tactics

Gulliver is also used to shock and embarrass us. He describes:

- Urinating and bowel movements all in graphic detail

- His being stripped naked and riding upon the nipple of a Maid of Honour

- The texture of skin and obscene eating habits in magnified detail

---

*not'* (p. 294) is not meant as a deception. In Part IV the **satirical** ingredient is sarcasm and the grey 'master' frequently uses this. He describes the Yahoo as '*a strange sort of animal*' (p. 267).

## GLUMDALCLITCH

Glumdalclitch is a child of nine who appears in Part II and acts as a carer for Gulliver. She acts as go-between for Gulliver in this land of Giants. She looks after him; she:

- Makes his clothes

- Teaches him some of the language

- Cares for his well-being

- Helps make him a bed

Glumdalclitch

Glumdalclitch regards Gulliver as her own and cares for him as a child would a doll, with tenderness and constant interest. Glumdalclitch is allowed to care for Gulliver at all times and is therefore allowed into court with him and to live with the queen. We are led to believe that Glumdalclitch is honest, moral and dedicated. She does tell tales of Gulliver's behaviour just as any nine-year-old would, but it is without malice, indeed she worships Gulliver and is heartbroken at the final parting.

**Lilliputian soldier**

# SETTINGS

## LILLIPUT

Lilliput is an island to the northwest of Australia separated from
Blefuscu by only a narrow strip of water, through which Gulliver is
able to wade. The capital of Lilliput is Mildendo.

Lilliput has a severe system of laws and punishment. People who are
traitors are put to death, as are people who wrongly accuse others.
Victims of false accusation are compensated. The law-abiding are
rewarded by being granted money or privileges at court. The statue
of Justice holds a bag of gold and a sheathed sword, symbolic of the
way in which peace is valued.

### Satire

Satire is introduced gradually in Lilliput – sometimes at Gulliver's
expense, but more often at the expense of the Lilliputians. Gulliver
is tied by 'slender ligatures' (p. 55) and while he is being fed he
considers himself 'bound by the laws of hospitality' (p. 59).

The Emperor is intended to represent King George I, who reigned
at Swift's time, and there are also many resemblances to King
George in the description of the King of Laputa, whom we meet
later.

Lilliput is portrayed as a miniature England of Swift's day. The
Emperor takes advice from his first minister as the King would have
taken advice from the Whigs. Intermittent warfare with Blefuscu
adds a sense of insecurity to the lives of the Lilliputians.

### The social strata of Lilliput

Gulliver takes pains to introduce us to social rank. He explains that
a Nardac is higher than a Clumglum. They all wear different
coloured threads to denote various honours that have been
bestowed upon them. Some of these honours are gained in the most
astonishing ways. There are competitions in creeping under or
leaping over a stick, rather like our high jump or limbo dancing.
There are also competitions in rope-dancing – these enable poor as

well as rich, educated as well as ignorant, to compete for honour.
The secretaries of state, we are told, accept money for their services.
We also are amazed that royal proclamations claim leniency has
been offered towards culprits, yet immediately there follow the
most severe sentences! Gulliver portrays a regime that wants to be
seen to be just, rather than one that is just.

### Divisions in Lilliput

The nation is divided into two political parties:

1. The Tramecksan, or High-Heels, who are the biggest party

2. The Slamecksan, or Low-Heels, who are actually in power

Amusingly, we are told that the heir to the throne, the young
prince, wears one of each shoe and hobbles between the two
parties. We are then introduced to:

1. Big-Endians, who follow the old religion and eat their eggs
   from the big end

2. Little-Endians, who have claimed freedom to interpret
   '*convenient end*' (p. 85), and open their eggs at the little end.

The two groups fight with each other about which end is the
correct one.

The people of Lilliput are presented to us en masse as spectators of
the massive Gulliver. We learn little of them except that they are
buried head-downwards because their expectation of life after death
is to be resurrected upside down.

### Children

We learn that children are educated in institutions that are suitable
for their intended careers, and that the children's handwriting slopes
from one corner to another. Designations are made at birth for the
type of education they will receive. The parents are expected to
make a contribution towards this education not simply by paying

**CHECKPOINT 36**

How hard is it
being a child in
Lilliput?

the school fees, but also by contributing towards their upkeep. In these institutions the children are prevented from having regular contact with their parents where they may be spoiled and bad habits develop, and are praised for their positive characteristics.

The boys and girls who will go into trade leave school earlier than the others into a kind of apprenticeship. Girls receive a more limited education than the boys, and are encouraged neither to wear jewellery nor to listen to gossip. The children of the labourers are not educated at all, but go to work as soon as they are old enough.

### Size and scale

Everyone and everything is one twelfth of the 'normal' size in Lilliput. Jonathan Swift has taken great care to scale down effectively all that we are asked to witness. Note how the snuffbox Gulliver owns is seen as a silver chest and his gun a hollow iron pillar. Gulliver's ticking watch makes a loud noise in Lilliput. Jonathan Swift cleverly contrasts the difference in size. He portrays Gulliver carrying tiny people, striding across their houses and being unable to see some tiny details of Lilliputian life. An example of this is someone threading a needle.

## BROBDINGNAG

The reader is led to believe that Brobdingnag is a 'continent' (p. 122) in the North Pacific, some 6,000 miles long with an impassable range of mountains bordering the country on one side, and a harbourless rocky coastline on the other.

**Gulliver meets the King**

Brobdingnag is a deliberate contrast to Lilliput. Here Gulliver finds himself one twelfth of the size of the inhabitants. Even the smallest animals are huge and terrifying for Gulliver. Gulliver has close encounters with dogs, cats, wasps, a monkey, a frog and a snail. He develops a sense of revulsion for all these enlarged encounters, and recalls faulty complexions, sores, a bloody execution, and even the act of someone eating. A suckling baby and a beggar repulse Gulliver, and he describes these events in graphic detail. This contrasts with Lilliput; begging does not take place and the sick and elderly are specially cared for by the State.

### Three-tier society

As a contrast to Lilliput, there are no political parties. Instead, there is simply a three-tier society of king, nobles and commoners (the working-class people). These common people display honest human weaknesses – greed and envy – and honest virtues, such as common sense, shrewdness and an avoidance of gossiping and trouble making. Everything here is very simplistic. The army is a left over from earlier civil wars; the libraries are sparse and few in number. The only subjects taught are morality, history, poetry and practical mathematics. Some of the cleverer individuals serve at court and advise the King.

### The King and government

Brobdingnag boasts a narrow-minded but practical King who listens patiently to Gulliver's description of England and makes careful notes before he cross-examines and questions him. Gulliver tries to respond as fully and as positively as he can to this questioning but the King arrives at his own conclusion: 'I cannot but conclude the bulk of your natives to be the most pernicious race of little odious vermin' (p. 173).

Despite this narrow-mindedness, the nation seems well governed and orderly. The King seems to concentrate on the physical realities rather than on political intrigue; he rules by the adage that he could 'make two ears of corn, or two blades of grass to grow upon a spot of ground where only one grew before' (p. 176). These simple people confound Gulliver in that they are unable to understand the notion of national debt or the variety of differences in religious or political opinions.

## LAPUTA

Swift used the third Part as a 'bridge' between the two almost ideal but opposite worlds of Brobdingnag and the land of the Houyhnhnms. Laputa is an island civilisation that floats through the air somewhere described vaguely as above the mid-Pacific. It is, we are told, a circular plate or saucer shape, three hundred yards thick and four-and-a-half miles in diameter. The underside of the island is reflective and smooth. Water gathers in the concave shape above to make four lakes, which provide drinking water.

**A scholar and his flapper**

**DID YOU KNOW?**

Swift seems to have made a prediction! The discovery of the two moons of Mars was not discovered in reality for another 150 years after *Gulliver's Travels* was published.

**DID YOU KNOW?**

Laputa seems to be a caricature of Japan (as it was perceived in the eighteenth century), its customs, learning and industry.

## Magnetism

The whole island is steered by a magnet, which is in the Astronomer's Cave and is six yards long. The motion is very smooth and, according to Gulliver, hardly noticeable. The magnet is caused by a set of controls either to be attracted or repulsed away from the earth's surface. The magnetic influence of the mineral below ground only works for up to four miles and does not work beyond the natural boundaries of the King's realm. This is useful in suppressing riots in neighbouring territories by parking above the territory and preventing the rain and sunshine reaching the ground below. The island people are also at liberty to bomb or even flatten those below them. This makes them a controlling power.

Laputa seems to have two main classes of people: commoners and another class which 'seemed to be of better quality' (p. 200). They have one eye turned inwards (introspective), and this makes them hold their heads on one side. The other eye is turned upward (astronomy). These people walk awkwardly and are clumsy because they are 'always so wrapped up in cogitation' (p. 201). For this reason, each person has a '*flapper*' (p. 201) to ensure their safety and to assist them in conversation.

## Music and mathematics

The people who inhabit this island are preoccupied with mathematics and music. Even the food they eat is carved into mathematical or instrumental shapes. Their preoccupation with the 'music of the spheres' (p. 204), often playing for three hours at a time, enables them to make very complex mathematical calculations. Frequently they get these calculations incorrect and this gives a bizarre appearance to everyday objects that are incorrectly designed. These mistakes include their houses, furniture and clothing.

Because these people are so absent-minded, they need servants called flappers whose job it is to smack their masters with a bladder to attract their attention. When they greet each other they are seldom relaxed, always anxious about the state of the Sun, fearing an eclipse or a comet. The women also seem tense and hate this very idle if comfortable life. The women are frequently visited by 'gallants' (p. 207) from the world below.

## BALNIBARBI

Balnibarbi lies on the main surface; it is larger than Laputa. Its capital is called Lagado. There is a poor picture painted of this place, with derelict housing and starving people. The agriculture has failed due to a series of misinformed projects, which took the place of the agriculture schemes which had been working well before the interference of Laputian scholars.

### Projectors

The leaders of these projects, called the projectors, have visited Laputa and are thought to understand the mathematical theories. They are very critical of people who stick to old-fashioned and traditional methods. The projectors are based in The Academy of Lagado. The academy has the reputation of housing senseless projects, for example:

- The extraction of sunshine from cucumbers
- The burning of ice to make gunpowder
- Building houses from the roof downwards
- Using blind people to mix paint
- Using pigs instead of manure
- Using cobwebs instead of silk
- Feeding coloured flies to the spiders to save on buying dye to colour the silks!

The whole theme is of contradictory elements; an attempt to condense air, sowing chaff instead of corn, growing wool-less sheep and making cushions of marble. These ideas are intended for us to question the real 'value' of the product.

> **GLOSSARY**
> **cogitation** thought

Inside the academy are various 'schools':

THE DEPARTMENT OF SPECULATIVE LEARNING: Here the academics debate continually over their fantastic and astonishing projects. Here we are introduced to the 'frame' (p. 227), which contains all the words in the language. These are tiny pieces of wood and are connected by wires onto handles. To change the order of the words, the handles are moved; if this turns up a logical sequence of words, the phrases are written down. All these phrases are saved and are to be put into a compendium of all the available knowledge; this produces a very mixed and jumbled language.

THE SCHOOL OF LANGUAGE: This peculiar school discards all words except nouns and uses objects instead of words in the 'universal language' (p. 231). The philosophy behind this is that it will save men's lives but they would need to travel to communicate effectively.

THE SCHOOL OF MATHEMATICS: A mathematical problem is solved and written down on a small biscuit called a 'wafer' (p. 231). The ink used is a fluid which can be absorbed by the brain. To eat these solutions means the natural absorption of mathematical knowledge takes place through the diet.

**CHECKPOINT 37**

What is Swift saying about politicians?

THE SCHOOL OF POLITICS: Ministers are appointed to this school by assessing their qualifications. Parliaments are likened to diseased bodies, and require a medical cure by regularly diagnosing and treating the Members of Parliament. In this school surgical fusion of half-brains in the same skull reconciles two schools of opinion and therefore brings a peaceful political reconciliation. Political posts are obtained by a raffle system. Instead of being an active politician, the election relies simply on good luck. Neighbours are invited to assess each other's vices; these vices are then taxed accordingly. Other equally peculiar features are included in this assessment such as whether or not women are good-looking and smartly dressed.

# GLUBBDUBDRIB

This is the land of magic and sorcerers and is referred to as 'The Island of *Sorcerers* or *Magicians*' (p. 238). The Prince is waited upon by dead servants, who are required to work for twenty-four hours every three months. These servants respond to questions, but only about their own lifetimes. They are unable to talk about any other event in history, and this frustrates Gulliver.

# LUGGNAGG

The capital of this country is Trildrogdrib. Here there is a strange custom where visitors to court are asked to lick the dust before the royal footstool. Favourable guests, like Gulliver, face a recently swept floor, whereas it is poisoned for those who are condemned.

The people in this land are courteous, good at conversing, and prefer even numbers to odd ones.

The Struldbruggs are born with a red spot over the left eye, which as they grow becomes green, blue and then black. These strange 'people' are said to be 'Immortals' (p. 252). They seem to be normal until thirty years of age, but then undergo a type of depression and lose any kind of regard for other people. They are jealous of the young, and recount exploits of their own youth. These exploits are frequently misremembered. These people are only able to estimate their age by the name of the last king before they entered into the Struldbrugg stage, which takes place at about eighty years of age. They long for death, especially when at the age of eighty they are separated from their spouses and are regarded as being officially 'dead' (p. 258). By the age of ninety they have declined; they are no longer able to read or converse, and they are seen as unpopular. This glimpse of longevity, and the pathetic figures it produces, horrifies Gulliver.

# THE LAND OF THE HOUYHNHNMS

The land is not portrayed in detail. The reader is given only a sketchy idea of what the country looks like with the mention of farm buildings, rivers and fields; in this part of the book the focus is on intellectuality.

**CHECKPOINT 38**

Which ghosts does Gulliver *choose* to meet?

**A Struldbrugg**

 **DID YOU KNOW?**

In his *Thoughts on Various Subjects*, Swift says that 'Every Man desires to live long; but no Man would be old.'

**Yahoo**

In this land we are introduced to two very different races:

YAHOOS: A savage version of human beings

HOUYHNHNMS: A superior breed of horses

The horses are the ruling species and attempt to communicate with Gulliver. The first horse Gulliver encounters is the grey horse who becomes his 'master' (p. 280). From this horse Gulliver learns that the horses are called Houyhnhnms (which incidentally sounds like a horse's whinny), and the savage humans who live wild in the bush are called Yahoos.

Gulliver lives here for about three years in a mud and wattle house erected for him by the Yahoos. The Houyhnhnms attempt to draw comparisons between themselves and their own form and that of Gulliver. They note his resemblance to the Yahoos, whom he comes to resemble even more when he is given fur and skins to wear instead of clothes. The horses feel that Gulliver smells like a Yahoo and that his clothes conceal his real identity. Gulliver persistently ignores the Yahoos, as he sees communication with these savages as a threat to his own safety.

Gulliver learns that the Houyhnhnms have a cultural background: they enjoy poetry, astronomy and have knowledge of herbal medicines. The Houyhnhnms are benevolent, kindly and are aware of the principles of friendship and good behaviour. These values are taught to the young who experience a regime of strict discipline. Lies are unknown and Gulliver takes trouble to explain what a lie is to them: they understand it as '*the thing which was not*' (p. 281). It is a strange moral issue that this exceptionally truthful species is not religious, has no faith and seemingly no real interest in the dilemmas faced by each other.

Now take a break!

## LANGUAGE AND STYLE

### GULLIVER AS NARRATOR

*Gulliver's Travels* is a first-person narrative: Gulliver tells us the story, interprets judgements for us, and helps us to form opinions. The use of the first person announces to the reader that this is how I, Jonathan Swift, see things through the eyes of my main character and storyteller. He is satirising the society in which his original readers lived, and they would have been able to sympathise directly with Gulliver.

As narrator, Gulliver's view is innocent, unemotional, clearly focused and unambiguous (see **ambiguity**). Pretending to be an innocent or even foreign visitor in a new land is a common enough device, since it enables the writer to reveal how the ordinary things that we take for granted are done in a way that will strike a foreigner as strange. This device may be used not only to poke fun, but also to invite the readers to look again at the things they take for granted.

At the same time as the observations, we are allowed an insight into Gulliver's (or Swift's) opinions. Gulliver, educated and rational, inspires our confidence from the first. He supplies us with detailed observations that add to the verisimilitude of the plot.

The difficulty for the reader of a text like this is that other characters remain ill defined and in the background. The plot is the strongest feature, from life with miniature men to the land of giants, to the land of academics and finally to the intellectuals. We are given not only the exciting action, but also Gulliver's reflections on what he hears and sees and also his views on life back home in England.

### SATIRE AND IRONY

Satire and irony run throughout all four Parts (see also **Themes** where the satirical style of *Gulliver's Travels* is dealt with). Jonathan Swift said:

> Satire is a sort of glass wherein beholders do generally discover everybody's face but their own; which is the chief reason ... that so very few are offended with it. (*Battle of Books*, 1696)

 **DID YOU KNOW?**
In one of his letters Swift wrote: 'Proper words in proper places make the true definitions of a style'.

**GLOSSARY**
glass mirror

It is his gentle use of adventure in criticising his England, Ireland, and government that makes Jonathan Swift's novel work on two levels.

Gulliver is used to deliver a technique of reversal or verbal irony. In Part I we are told of the Emperor's qualities, all of which are the opposite of George I's characteristics. In Part II Gulliver's praise of his country is over-exaggerated, and therefore lacks credibility. Very often, one seemingly credible paragraph is followed by another that makes us reconsider what we have already read. This is a particular device in Part IV which engages the reader to reflect upon what is written. An example of this is when Gulliver explains what horses are used in for in England and shocks the Houyhnhnms.

Other examples of irony are easy to identify as the italicised words show:

> I was demanded to swear to the performance of them; first in the manner of my own country, and afterwards in the method prescribed by their laws (p. 78)

> These *unhappy* people were proposing schemes for persuading monarchs to choose favourites upon the score of their wisdom, capacity and virtue (p. 232)

> The last of these (mathematics) is wholly applied to what may be useful in life, to the improvement of agriculture and all mechanical arts; so *that among us it would be little esteemed.* (p. 176)

There are also many examples of sarcasm:

> And it would be *hard* indeed, if so *remote* a Prince's notions of virtue and vice were to be offered as a standard for all mankind. (p. 174)

The language seems strange to our ears, particularly the descriptions of life at sea, which are portrayed in so much detail. However the story transcends three hundred years and the language does not inhibit our understanding of what is happening.

**DID YOU KNOW?**
In 1926 T. S. Eliot named Swift 'the greatest writer of English prose'

# HUMOUR

Satire and irony are often used to attack contemporary institutions in a humorous way. The two great political parties of Swift's day were the Whigs and the Tories and they put in an appearance in Part I Chapter 4, when the difference between the Tramecksans and the Slamecksans is described.

The parties are distinguished, he says, by the height of their heels, yet the difference between them is little more than a *'drurr'*, which is 'about the fourteenth part of an inch' (p. 84). He exploits this negligible difference and follows through the humorous possibilities by turning to an observation of the heir to the throne, who has a tendency towards the 'High-Heels' since he walks with a limp, a 'hobble in his gait' (p. 47), one heel being higher than the other! It is generally believed that this is a reference to the Prince of Wales who later became George II (1727–60). Before he became king, he was apparently favourable towards the Tories but once on the throne, he retained the Whigs in power under Walpole; and the image reflects his shifting loyalties.

The reader can enjoy the joke about the way minuscule differences between people can become great and significant causes for argument. Swift, however, completes the amusement for us by relating this to the political system. There is an additional pleasure for us when we apply what Swift has to say to our own political system and the apparently negligible differences between the different parties.

As well as satire and irony, Swift employs another level of humour: nonsense words – e.g. Big-Endians, Little-Endians, Struldbruggs, Tramecksans, Slamecksans, Yahoos – deliberate inventions which add a little humour, as well as a sense of mystery. Nonsense words also lend credibility to the bizarre story. It is well to remember that at the time of the publication, readers actually believed the stories and frequently looked up the islands in their atlases.

We might also derive amusement from the nonsensical ideas of the Laputans. Not only do they provide ludicrous solutions to their

**? DID YOU KNOW?**
Swift called books 'the children of the brain'

social problems (see III.4); they also carry out the most bizarre research projects. At the Academy of Lagado we find, for example, the hope of 'extracting sunbeams out of cucumbers' (p. 223) and attempts 'to calcine ice into gunpowder' (p. 224).

A more basic level of humour is derived from Gulliver's description of the way Projectors in the Academy of Lagado deal with his 'small fit of the colic' (p. 226). This is a treatment which involves rather brutally filling the bowels with air and water and awaiting the consequences! Not for the faint-hearted one would have thought, yet such a treatment is used to this day and the wealthy will pay good money for it (it is known as colonic irrigation).

The comic episodes in *Gulliver's Travels* remind us that great literature may be hard work at times for the reader but the study is amply repaid by the sheer enjoyment it invariably provides.

Some critics feel that there may be a similarity with the *Odyssey* by Homer (c.750BC) or *Tom Jones* by Henry Fielding (1749). *Gulliver's Travels* may be likened to Christian's journey in *The Pilgrim's Progress* (1684) and Robinson Crusoe's adventures (1719), but none of these display the deep satire, irony and humour of this unique text.

**CHECK THE NET**
www.jaffebros.
com/lee/gulliver/
index.html is one
of the most
comprehensive
websites on
*Gulliver's Travels*.

**Now take a break!**

## PART FOUR

## RESOURCES

# HOW TO USE QUOTATIONS

One of the secrets of success in writing essays is the way you use quotations. There are five basic principles:

1. Put inverted commas at the beginning and end of the quotation.
2. Write the quotation exactly as it appears in the original.
3. Do not use a quotation that repeats what you have just written.
4. Use the quotation so that it fits into your sentence.
5. Keep the quotation as short as possible.

Quotations should be used to develop the line of thought in your essays. Your comment should not duplicate what is in your quotation. For example:

> **When Gulliver awakes he tells us that 'The chains that held my left leg were about two yards long, and gave me not only the liberty of walking backwards and forwards in a semicircle but ...'**

Far more effective is to write:

> **Gulliver wakens and finds he is chained by his left leg and is able to walk 'backwards and forwards in a semicircle'.**

However, the most sophisticated way of using the writer's words is to embed them into your sentence:

> **Gulliver's 'liberty' was restricted as he was chained by his left leg.**

When you use quotations in this way, you are demonstrating the ability to use text as evidence to support your ideas – not simply including words from the original to prove you have read it.

**EXAMINER'S SECRET**

In a typical examination essay you might use as many as eight quotations.

**EXAMINER'S SECRET**

Short, snappy quotations are always the best.

**EXAMINER'S SECRET**

Examiners **never** take marks away.

**EXAMINER'S SECRET**

If you are asked to make a comparison, use comparing words such as, 'on the other hand', 'however' and 'by contrast'.

# COURSEWORK ESSAY

Set aside an hour or so at the start of your work to plan what you have to do.

- List all the points you feel are needed to cover the task. Collect page references of information and quotations that will support what you have to say. A helpful tool is the **highlighter pen**: this saves painstaking copying and enables you to target precisely what you want to use.

- Focus on what you consider to be the main points of the essay. Try to sum up your argument in a single sentence, which could be the closing sentence of your essay. Depending on the essay title, it could be a statement about a character: **Gulliver starts out as a naive but educated man, but finishes disillusioned and mentally disturbed;** an opinion about setting: **the more extraordinary the setting the more realistic the characters and plot;** or a judgement on a theme: *Gulliver's Travels* is simply a satirical comedy.

- Make a short essay plan. Use the first paragraph to introduce the argument you wish to make. In the following paragraphs develop this argument with details, examples and other possible points of view. Sum up your argument in the last paragraph. Check you have answered the question.

- Write the essay, remembering all the time the central point you are making.

- On completion, go back over what you have written to eliminate careless errors and improve expression. Read it aloud to yourself, or, if you are feeling more confident, to a relative or friend.

If you can, try to type your essay, using a word processor. This will allow you to correct and improve your writing without spoiling its appearance.

# SITTING THE EXAMINATION

Examination papers are carefully designed to give you the opportunity to do your best. Follow these handy hints for exam success:

## BEFORE YOU START

- Make sure you know the subject of the examination so that you are properly prepared and equipped.

- You need to be comfortable and free from distractions. Inform the invigilator if anything is off-putting, e.g. a shaky desk.

- Read the instructions, or rubric, on the front of the examination paper. You should know by now what you have to do but check to reassure yourself.

- Observe the time allocation – and follow it carefully. If they recommend 60 minutes for Question 1 and 30 minutes for Question 2, it is because Question 1 carries twice as many marks.

- Consider the mark allocation. You should write a longer response for 4 marks than for 2 marks.

## WRITING YOUR RESPONSES

- Use the questions to structure your response, e.g. question: 'The endings of X's poems are always particularly significant. Explain their importance with reference to two poems.' The first part of your answer will describe the ending of the first poem; the second part will look at the ending of the second poem; the third part will be an explanation of the significance of the two endings.

- Write a brief draft outline of your response.

- A typical 30-minute examination essay is probably between 400 and 600 words in length.

- Keep your writing legible and easy to read, using paragraphs to show the structure of your answers.

**EXAMINER'S SECRET**
Beware of feeling you have to finish an answer because you have reached the bottom of the page.

**EXAMINER'S SECRET**
Don't waste time looking to see how your friends are doing!

**EXAMINER'S SECRET**

Always have a spare pen!

- Spend a couple of minutes afterwards quickly checking for obvious errors.

## WHEN YOU HAVE FINISHED

- Don't be downhearted – if you found the examination difficult, it is probably because you really worked at the questions. Let's face it, they are not meant to be easy!

- Don't pay too much attention to what your friends have to say about the paper. Everyone's experience is different and no two people ever give the same answers.

## IMPROVE YOUR GRADE

Your potential grades in any examination can always be improved. Every candidate everywhere starts at the same point: a blank answer booklet. An examiner marks your work according to a mark scheme that is applied to all candidates and no examiner knows in advance your level of achievement.

You must realise that the examination board has determined that your answer book contains more than enough space for any candidate to get the highest marks so there is no need to rush your writing in order to fill up three or four extra sheets!

**EXAMINER'S SECRET**

Keep an eye on the clock so you do not run out of time.

Moreover, the examination board knows that the two hours your examination is scheduled to last is enough for a candidate to secure the highest marks without rushing. You are not expected to write solidly for two hours since the examiner confidently believes that you will spend at least some of the time thinking!

So take your time. Think carefully, plan carefully, write carefully and check carefully. A relaxed performer always works best – in any field and in every examination!

Whatever you are studying, the way to be completely at ease with it in an examination is to know it inside out. There is no substitute for reading and re-reading the text.

The main reason that candidates let themselves down in the examination room is that they fail to read the question! Do not begin writing until you are quite sure what you want to say because it is very easy to lose track and end up writing off the subject. Whilst you are writing, it is a good idea to check back occasionally to the question and satisfy yourself that you are still answering it.

Keep an eye on the clock. Most literature papers require you to answer two questions in two hours. It may seem obvious but it is worth reminding yourself that to do yourself justice you need to spend about an hour on each question! This is all the more important when you feel happier answering one question rather than the other. If you steal time to produce a lengthy answer on one question, you are far more likely to lose all the extra marks you have gained by handing in a feeble response for the question you did not like.

Let's look at ways of different candidates may *start* their responses to the following question:

> **Why does Swift write at length about Gulliver's visit to the Academy of Lagado?**

## GRADE D OR E

A candidate will concentrate on literal evidence. S/he will offer simple descriptions of the experiments Gulliver witnesses and offer simple statements in straightforward comments:

> **Gulliver sees a lot of experiments taking place in the academy. In one place a man is trying to make cobwebs into fabric that will be cheaper and finer than silk. He thinks the scientists are stupid when they try to soften marble so that it can be used for pillows. They are even more stupid when they use a blind man to mix colours for painters so that they can tell the difference between colours by their feel or smell. Gulliver thinks the scientists are stupid.**

This is a very simple answer. The candidate will be rewarded for knowledge of the text but they would need to provide more

**EXAMINER'S SECRET**
Spend most time on questions that offer most marks.

**EXAMINER'S SECRET**
Always read the whole examination paper before you start writing.

comment supported by evidence quoted from the text if they wanted to gain higher marks.

## GRADE C OR B

A candidate will pay more attention to the question, quoting from the book and attempting to offer some judgements:

> **Gulliver is taken on an amusing guided tour of the Academy of Lagado and sees various experiments in action. First, he watches a man with 'meagre aspect, with sooty hands and face' (p. 223) who is trying to extract 'sunbeams out of cucumbers' (p. 223). This is clearly a foolish occupation and the purpose – 'to supply the Governor's gardens with sunshine at a reasonable rate' (pp. 223–4) – is as unlikely as it is laughable. Next he is taken to a 'chamber' where a man is attempting to 'reduce human excrement to its original food' (p. 224). The man gives him a 'very close embrace' and Swift makes us laugh when he says it is 'a compliment I could well have excused' (p. 224). Again we feel that the man is wasting his time on a very unpleasant task. This is all the more true since, by definition, excrement is human waste so there will be no goodness in anything he manages to produce in any case!**

This is a much better response than the literal description of Gulliver's visit. The candidate is attempting to answer the question and using quotations to support the commentary. There are attempts to explain the humour and a personal comment is offered. However, this sort of treatment is obviously going to result in a very long essay since there are another twenty or so different experiments to consider. It is worth noting that a more focused answer will be achieved by rigorous planning of what experiments will be included in the essay and which are worthy of quotation.

## GRADE A OR A*

The candidate assumes that the examiner knows the text. S/he will not spend time writing an account of the visit but concentrate on bringing out the writer's methods and achievements:

Gulliver's visit to the academy occupies a couple of brilliantly funny chapters. He sees a variety of unlikely experiments: a man trying to get sunshine out of cucumbers, another who is practising a primitive form of colonic irrigation with bellows that have 'a long, slender muzzle' delicately fashioned from 'ivory' (p. 226) which is presumably smooth enough for its unpleasant purpose!

Other so-called 'projectors' are engaged on other projects such as reducing language to *'things'* that may be flourished around like objects, cut out unnecessary talking and, more importantly, provide a 'universal language' (p. 231). Gulliver notes in passing that whilst men would be happy with this form of communication, women along with 'vulgar and illiterate' people have objected to not being allowed 'the liberty to speak with their tongues' (p. 230).

The humour is wide-ranging and cleverly developed but you realise the cleverness of Swift's imagination when you know that in his time there were any number of attempts to introduce a universal language. You also reflect that Swift hits upon exactly those sorts of things that are always true of humanity. Great writing is always true.

This response shows the ability to integrate comment, description and reference. The quotations show that the writer has fully absorbed what is written into his or her own thinking.

There is no attempt here to write a blow-by-blow account of the text: the candidate has a view of the whole visit and the response ranges comfortably across the two chapters.

There is a real attempt to be precise by careful choice of vocabulary: 'a primitive form', 'delicately fashioned', 'this form of communication'. The writer is also trying to draw a wider point from what s/he has read: that these chapters illustrate the 'cleverness of Swift's imagination'. In these words s/he sums up exactly why Swift does write at length about Gulliver's visit to the academy.

**EXAMINER'S SECRET**
If the rubric gives planning time, **use it** to plan your answers!

**EXAMINER'S SECRET**
You can get top marks in an English examination with two sides of writing.

## SAMPLE ESSAY PLAN

A typical essay question on *Gulliver's Travels* is followed by a
sample essay plan in note form. You will need to look back through
the text to find quotations to support your points. Think about
your own ideas – the sample answer is only a suggestion and you
may wish to ignore it and produce your own. But it is always a
good idea to plan out your thoughts first – it will save you time and
help you to organise your ideas. Remember – try to answer the
question!

> '*Gulliver's Travels* is a simple story, simply told for young
> children.' Discuss.

The essay falls into two main parts: yes, it is, and no, not just for
young children. This works on two levels, an exciting adventure and
a deep satire.

## A: YES

Young children enjoy the lively adventures. Look for what would
be pleasing for them:

| | |
|---|---|
| Lilliput: | ● The tiny people |
| | ● The 'interview at court' |
| | ● The way practicalities are dealt with, i.e. food and drink and a bed for Gulliver |
| Brobdingnag: | ● The concern young readers would have for the tiny Gulliver's safety |
| | ● The encounters with dog, boy, cat and wasps |
| Laputa: | ● The weird inhabitants and their obsessions with experiments |
| Balnibarbi: | ● Sympathy for the people who live in the shadow of Laputa |
| Glubbdubdrib/ Luggnagg: | ● The horror of being waited upon by dead people and, even worse, people forever waiting for death |

Gulliver portrays all of these scenes in a very graphic and colourful way.

## 3: No

This book is meant for an adult audience. It is a satire by Jonathan Swift on the life and times he experiences. The events in the four Parts reflect Jonathan Swift's view of humanity. The reader needs to understand the historical background in order to really gain the full appreciation of this text. Issues to be explored in this part of the essay are:

Politics:
- Whigs and Tories represented by Slamecksans and Tramecksans

Church:
- The problems of differences of opinion in Lilliput and Blefuscu

Anglo-Irish problems:
- Reflected in the journey from Laputa to Balnibarbi, the nation of absentee landlords and neglect
- Scientific research and The Royal Society
- Laputa

**EXAMINER'S SECRET**
Plan your answers – then you will not repeat yourself.

## FURTHER QUESTIONS

Make a plan as shown above and attempt these questions.

1. *Gulliver's Travels* is about the decline of humanity into savagery. What evidence is there in the text to support this idea?

2. How successful is *Gulliver's Travels*? Are Parts I and II more believable than Parts III and IV? If so, why?

3. Using *Gulliver's Travels*, identify what Jonathan Swift considered to be good government and the ideas he identified as being those of poor government.

4. Gulliver is tested in a variety of ways; what does this tell the reader about his character?

**CHECK THE BOOK**
See if you can get hold of *Gulliver's Travels: A Critical Study* by W. A. Eddy (Princeton University Press, 1923).

⑤ It is said that Swift found 'much that was ugly, little that was beautiful'. Using *Gulliver's Travels* find evidence for this statement.

⑥ Compare the exploration of human nature in *Gulliver's Travels* with that portrayed by either:
a   *An Inspector Calls* by J. B. Priestley (1945)
b   *Journey's End* by R. C. Sherriff (1929)
c   *Blood Brothers* by Willy Russell (1985)
d   *Animal Farm* by George Orwell (1945)
e   *To Kill a Mockingbird* by Harper Lee (1960)
f   *Lord of the Flies* by William Golding (1954)

⑦ Compare the exploration of authority and hierarchical structures in *Gulliver's Travels* with either:
a   *Journey's End* by R. C. Sherriff (1929)
b   *Talking in Whispers* by James Watson (1983)
c   *Of Mice and Men* by John Steinbeck (1937)
d   *Lord of the Flies* by William Golding (1954)

⑧ Compare the use of satire and irony in *Gulliver's Travels* with either:
a   *An Inspector Calls* by J. B. Priestley (1945)
b   *Animal Farm* by George Orwell (1945)

⑨ Compare the BBC video presentation of *Gulliver* with the text. Do you feel Gulliver is portrayed more favourably in one than the other?

**CHECK THE FILM**

Cartoon Crazys have produced a carton version of *Gulliver's Travels* which is available to buy on video.

⑩ Compare the way the fantasy of *Gulliver's Travels* is treated with one of the following:
a   *Alice in Wonderland* by Lewis Carroll (1862)
b   *The Queen and I* by Sue Townsend (1992)
c   *The Borrowers* by Mary Norton (1966)

ambiguity to have a double meaning

denote to signify or mark out

device any literary method or technique can be called a device

irony saying one thing whilst meaning another (see **Satire** in **Themes**)

narrator the storyteller

parody an imitation designed to mock or ridicule

satire a literary work in which vices, follies, stupidities, abuses for example are held up to ridicule and contempt

symbol where one thing is used to act or stand for another

verisimilitude the believability of a sequence or story

# CHECKPOINT HINTS/ANSWERS

CHECKPOINT 1 We learn that Gulliver is an educated man from a respectable home, thus we are more likely to trust his account. Also, his background strongly contrasts with the lands he will visit.

CHECKPOINT 2 They seem aggressive, but it is important to remember that he is twelve times their size! However, note that it is Gulliver who feels powerless.

CHECKPOINT 3 They tie him up, then attack him with arrows. Why do they begin to treat him more kindly?

CHECKPOINT 4 Notice how the Emperor keeps his distance and consider the searches made when Gulliver enters the Court, and the confiscation of his possessions.

CHECKPOINT 5 Swift is saying that promotions are not always based on merit.

CHECKPOINT 6 Check back to p. 78.

CHECKPOINT 7 It reminds us that Gulliver is writing a travelogue. What is your first impression of Maldendo?

CHECKPOINT 8 They are not allowed to hold office and their books are banned from Lilliput.

CHECKPOINT 9
- His refusal to destroy Blefescu completely
- His friendliness towards the ambassadors from Blefescu
- His urinating on the palace

CHECKPOINT 10 Working-class children leave school and start apprenticeships when they are seven years old (though some girls stay at school till they are elecven). Upper-class boys stay at school till they are fifteen and upper-class girls leave school when they are twelve years old.

CHECKPOINT 11 Flimnap, the Lord High Treasurer recommends that Gulliver is dismissed for two reasons. What are they? Flimnap is 'a favourite' of the Emperor (p. 103), who is swayed by his opinions.

CHECKPOINT 12 Consider:
- Gulliver's actions
- His attitude towards Blefuscu
- His attitude towards Lilliput

CHECKPOINT 13 Yes. Consider his response to the welcome given by the Monarch of Blefuscu.

CHECKPOINT 14 Whereas the Emperor of Lilliput treats Gulliver with suspicion and then turns against him, the Emperor of Blefuscu is kind and courteous, welcoming Gulliver and assisting him in his journey home.

CHECKPOINT 15
- Gulliver's master exploits him for money.
- The Queen and her attendants are 'delighted' by him (p. 139).
- Glumdaliclitch is overjoyed to be able to stay with Gulliver at the palace.
- At first, the King thinks Gulliver is a *splacknuck* or a clockwork toy.
- Look at the scholars' suggestions on pp. 142–3.

CHECKPOINT 16 Find the passage relating to Maldendo (1.4) and compare the descriptions of the two cities.

CHECKPOINT 17 It is much bigger, so that Gulliver has to climb up and down a ladder to read them! However, the book contains 'the usual topics of European moralists' (p. 178).

CHECKPOINT 18 He finds it strange to be back with people of the same size as himself. His family and the houses seem tiny to him now and he feels like 'a giant' (p. 191).

CHECKPOINT 19 In both Lilliput and Brobdingnag. Can you remember the circumstances? Look for this later in the book too.

CHECKPOINT 20 Compare the role of women here and in Lilliput.

CHECKPOINT 21 Gulliver was conscious of his size in Parts I and II. It has clearly had a profound effect on him!

CHECKPOINT 22 Read p. 225 again to find out.

CHECKPOINT 23 Look back to p. 241 and make sure you know why they are important.

CHECKPOINT 24 Swift wants to emphasise the contrasts in their lifestyles. How do they compare?

CHECKPOINT 25 At first the idea of immortality fills Gulliver with 'rapture' and 'delight' until he realises that it must be accompanied by old age.

CHECKPOINT 26 It is unlikely that Gulliver would have been accepted into Japan and the whole chapter gives very little detail, especially about his family.

CHECKPOINT 27 He has spent a happy five months at home with his family. When he is marooned, Gulliver describes his 'desolate condition' (p. 268).

CHECKPOINT 28
- He addresses them as 'Gentlemen' and 'your Worships' (p. 272) – he sees the horses as superior.
- Gulliver thinks they might be human magicians but the Houyhnhnms cannot understand a word he says.

CHECKPOINT 29 The Houyhnhnm is surprised that someone who looks like a Yahoo is so easy to teach, but does not believe that the intelligence he demonstrates is real.

CHECKPOINT 30
- The master has 'much difficulty' (p. 286) in understanding the lies, doubts and deceit that Gulliver talks about because their communication deals with 'facts' alone.
- He shows 'great indignation' (p. 287) when he hears that humans are superior to horses, and 'noble resentment' (p. 288) about the way in which horses are treated.
- He says that Gulliver 'differed for the worse' (p. 288) from the Houyhnhnms in his physical appearance.
- He shows 'amazement and indignation' (p. 291) when he is able to understand government, power, crime and law etc.

CHECKPOINT 31 Although both humans and Yahoos are capable of 'brutality', Yahoos could not be blamed for it, because it comes naturally to them. Humans on the other hand pretend to possess reason, and so the results of the brutality are worse.

CHECKPOINT 32 Look at p. 301.

CHECKPOINT 33 He says he will be useful to humans 'by celebrating the praises of renowned Houyhnhnms, and proposing their virtues to the imitation of mankind' (p. 329).

CHECKPOINT 34 He is not very successful at all. Five years later, Gulliver still prefers to spend time with horses than with his family.

CHECKPOINT 35 Take into account Gulliver's claims in IV.12, and think about the different opinions of Swift and Gulliver.

CHECKPOINT 36 Think about age, gender and class differences and the fact that children are educated away from their families.

CHECKPOINT 37  Perhaps that they are all diseased.

CHECKPOINT 38  Gulliver mentions a good many in IV.7 and 8. How many of them are from classical times?

## TEST YOURSELF (PART I)

1 Gulliver (*Chapter 1*)

2 The Hurgo (*Chapter 1*)

3 The great gate of the temple (*Chapter 1*)

4 The Emperor (*Chapter 2*)

5 Filmnap (*Chapter 3*)

6 Reldresal (*Chapter 4*)

7 Mildendo (*Chapter 4*)

8 Tramecksan (*Chapter 4*)

9 Blefuscudians (*Chapter 5*)

## TEST YOURSELF (PART II)

1 The Farmer (*Chapter 1*)

2 Glumdalclitch (*Chapter 2*)

3 The Farmer (*Chapter 3*)

4 The King of Brobdingnag (*Chapter 3*)

5 The Queen of Brobdingnag (*Chapter 5*)

## TEST YOURSELF (PART III)

1 Captain William Robinson (*Chapter 1*)

2 The Dutchman (*Chapter 1*)

3 Laputa (*Chapter 1*)

4 Laputians (*Chapter 2*)

5 A Flapper (*Chapter 2*)

6 The Academy (*Chapter 5*)

7 Glubbdubdrib (*Chapter 7*)

8 Luggnaggians (*Chapter 10*)

9 Struldbruggs (*Chapter 10*)

## TEST YOURSELF (PART IV)

1 Captain Pocock of Bristol (*Chapter 1*)

2 Gulliver's wife (*Chapter 1*)

3 The Yahoos (*Chapter 1*)

4 The Houyhnhnms (*Chapter 1*)

5 The Houyhnhnms (*Chapter 9*)

6 Don Pedro (*Chapter 11*)

7 Gulliver's wife and family (*Chapter 11*)

# NOTES

# NOTES

Maya Angelou
*I Know Why the Caged Bird Sings*

Jane Austen
*Pride and Prejudice*

Alan Ayckbourn
*Absent Friends*

Elizabeth Barrett Browning
*Selected Poems*

Robert Bolt
*A Man for All Seasons*

Harold Brighouse
*Hobson's Choice*

Charlotte Brontë
*Jane Eyre*

Emily Brontë
*Wuthering Heights*

Shelagh Delaney
*A Taste of Honey*

Charles Dickens
*David Copperfield*
*Great Expectations*
*Hard Times*
*Oliver Twist*

Roddy Doyle
*Paddy Clarke Ha Ha Ha*

George Eliot
*Silas Marner*
*The Mill on the Floss*

Anne Frank
*The Diary of a Young Girl*

William Golding
*Lord of the Flies*

Oliver Goldsmith
*She Stoops to Conquer*

Willis Hall
*The Long and the Short and the Tall*

Thomas Hardy
*Far from the Madding Crowd*

*The Mayor of Casterbridge*
*Tess of the d'Urbervilles*
*The Withered Arm and other Wessex Tales*

L.P. Hartley
*The Go-Between*

Seamus Heaney
*Selected Poems*

Susan Hill
*I'm the King of the Castle*

Barry Hines
*A Kestrel for a Knave*

Louise Lawrence
*Children of the Dust*

Harper Lee
*To Kill a Mockingbird*

Laurie Lee
*Cider with Rosie*

Arthur Miller
*The Crucible*
*A View from the Bridge*

Robert O'Brien
*Z for Zachariah*

Frank O'Connor
*My Oedipus Complex and Other Stories*

George Orwell
*Animal Farm*

J.B. Priestley
*An Inspector Calls*
*When We Are Married*

Willy Russell
*Educating Rita*
*Our Day Out*

J.D. Salinger
*The Catcher in the Rye*

William Shakespeare
*Henry IV Part I*
*Henry V*
*Julius Caesar*
*Macbeth*

*The Merchant of Venice*
*A Midsummer Night's Dream*
*Much Ado About Nothing*
*Romeo and Juliet*
*The Tempest*
*Twelfth Night*

George Bernard Shaw
*Pygmalion*

Mary Shelley
*Frankenstein*

R.C. Sherriff
*Journey's End*

Rukshana Smith
*Salt on the snow*

John Steinbeck
*Of Mice and Men*

Robert Louis Stevenson
*Dr Jekyll and Mr Hyde*

Jonathan Swift
*Gulliver's Travels*

Robert Swindells
*Daz 4 Zoe*

Mildred D. Taylor
*Roll of Thunder, Hear My Cry*

Mark Twain
*Huckleberry Finn*

James Watson
*Talking in Whispers*

Edith Wharton
*Ethan Frome*

William Wordsworth
*Selected Poems*

*A Choice of Poets*

*Mystery Stories of the Nineteenth Century including The Signalman*

*Nineteenth Century Short Stories*

*Poetry of the First World War*

*Six Women Poets*

Margaret Atwood
*Cat's Eye*
*The Handmaid's Tale*

Jane Austen
*Emma*
*Mansfield Park*
*Persuasion*
*Pride and Prejudice*
*Sense and Sensibility*

Alan Bennett
*Talking Heads*

William Blake
*Songs of Innocence and of Experience*

Charlotte Brontë
*Jane Eyre*
*Villette*

Emily Brontë
*Wuthering Heights*

Angela Carter
*Nights at the Circus*

Geoffrey Chaucer
*The Franklin's Prologue and Tale*
*The Miller's Prologue and Tale*
*The Prologue to the Canterbury Tales*
*The Wife of Bath's Prologue and Tale*

Samuel Coleridge
*Selected Poems*

Joseph Conrad
*Heart of Darkness*

Daniel Defoe
*Moll Flanders*

Charles Dickens
*Bleak House*
*Great Expectations*
*Hard Times*

Emily Dickinson
*Selected Poems*

John Donne
*Selected Poems*

Carol Ann Duffy
*Selected Poems*

George Eliot
*Middlemarch*
*The Mill on the Floss*

T.S. Eliot
*Selected Poems*
*The Waste Land*

F. Scott Fitzgerald
*The Great Gatsby*

E.M. Forster
*A Passage to India*

Brian Friel
*Translations*

Thomas Hardy
*Jude the Obscure*
*The Mayor of Casterbridge*
*The Return of the Native*
*Selected Poems*
*Tess of the d'Urbervilles*

Seamus Heaney
*Selected Poems from 'Opened Ground'*

Nathaniel Hawthorne
*The Scarlet Letter*

Homer
*The Iliad*
*The Odyssey*

Aldous Huxley
*Brave New World*

Kazuo Ishiguro
*The Remains of the Day*

Ben Jonson
*The Alchemist*

James Joyce
*Dubliners*

John Keats
*Selected Poems*

Christopher Marlowe
*Doctor Faustus*
*Edward II*

Arthur Miller
*Death of a Salesman*

John Milton
*Paradise Lost Books I & II*

Toni Morrison
*Beloved*

George Orwell
*Nineteen Eighty-Four*

Sylvia Plath
*Selected Poems*

Alexander Pope
*Rape of the Lock & Selected Poems*

William Shakespeare
*Antony and Cleopatra*
*As You Like It*
*Hamlet*
*Henry IV Part I*
*King Lear*
*Macbeth*
*Measure for Measure*
*The Merchant of Venice*
*A Midsummer Night's Dream*
*Much Ado About Nothing*
*Othello*
*Richard II*
*Richard III*
*Romeo and Juliet*
*The Taming of the Shrew*
*The Tempest*
*Twelfth Night*
*The Winter's Tale*

George Bernard Shaw
*Saint Joan*

Mary Shelley
*Frankenstein*

Jonathan Swift
*Gulliver's Travels and A Modest Proposal*

Alfred Tennyson
*Selected Poems*

Virgil
*The Aeneid*

Alice Walker
*The Color Purple*

Oscar Wilde
*The Importance of Being Earnest*

Tennessee Williams
*A Streetcar Named Desire*

Jeanette Winterson
*Oranges Are Not the Only Fruit*

John Webster
*The Duchess of Malfi*

Virginia Woolf
*To the Lighthouse*

W.B. Yeats
*Selected Poems*

*Metaphysical Poets*

At York Notes we believe in helping you achieve exam success. Log on to **www.yorknotes.com** and see how we have made revision even easier, with over 300 titles available to download twenty-four hours a day. The downloads have lots of additional features such as pop-up boxes providing instant glossary definitions, user-friendly links to every part of the guide, and scanned illustrations offering visual appeal. All you need to do is log on to **www.yorknotes.com** and download the books you need to help you achieve exam success.

## KEY FEATURES:

Details on how York Notes can help you

Menu Bar to help you find your way around the site

Details on how to download York Notes

Quick Search facility to help you find the titles you need

Link to news about new titles

List of top-selling downloads

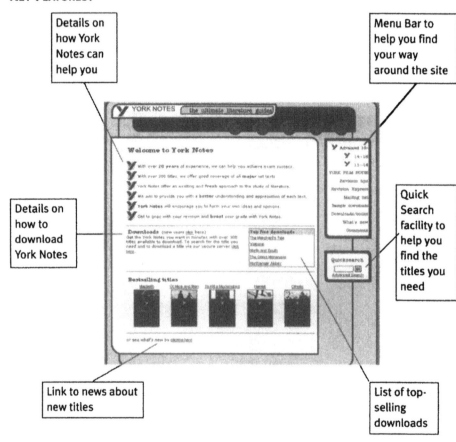